THE POCKET IDIOT'S GUIDE™ TO

The FairTax

by Ken Clark, CFP

ALPHA

A member of Penguin Group (USA) Inc.

To every taxpayer who has tried to navigate the system with integrity but is officially burnt out and ready to discuss change.

ALPHA BOOKS

Published by the Penguin Group

Penguin Group (USA) Inc., 375 Hudson Street, New York, New York 10014, USA

Penguin Group (Canada), 90 Eglinton Avenue East, Suite 700, Toronto, Ontario M4P 2Y3, Canada (a division of Pearson Penguin Canada Inc.)

Penguin Books Ltd., 80 Strand, London WC2R 0RL, England

Penguin Ireland, 25 St. Stephen's Green, Dublin 2, Ireland (a division of Penguin Books Ltd.)

Penguin Group (Australia), 250 Camberwell Road, Camberwell, Victoria 3124, Australia (a division of Pearson Australia Group Pty. Ltd.)

Penguin Books India Pvt. Ltd., 11 Community Centre, Panchsheel Park, New Delhi—110 017, India

Penguin Group (NZ), 67 Apollo Drive, Rosedale, North Shore, Auckland 1311, New Zealand (a division of Pearson New Zealand Ltd.)

Penguin Books (South Africa) (Pty.) Ltd., 24 Sturdee Avenue, Rosebank, Johannesburg 2196, South Africa

Penguin Books Ltd., Registered Offices: 80 Strand, London WC2R 0RL, England

International Standard Book Number: 978-1-59257-956-3
Library of Congress Catalog Card Number: 2009932858

12 11 10   8 7 6 5 4 3 2 1

Interpretation of the printing code: The rightmost number of the first series of numbers is the year of the book's printing; the rightmost number of the second series of numbers is the number of the book's printing. For example, a printing code of 10-1 shows that the first printing occurred in 2010.

Printed in the United States of America

Note: This publication contains the opinions and ideas of its author. It is intended to provide helpful and informative material on the subject matter covered. It is sold with the understanding that the author and publisher are not engaged in rendering professional services in the book. If the reader requires personal assistance or advice, a competent professional should be consulted.

The author and publisher specifically disclaim any responsibility for any liability, loss, or risk, personal or otherwise, which is incurred as a consequence, directly or indirectly, of the use and application of any of the contents of this book.

Most Alpha books are available at special quantity discounts for bulk purchases for sales promotions, premiums, fund-raising, or educational use. Special books, or book excerpts, can also be created to fit specific needs.

For details, write: Special Markets, Alpha Books, 375 Hudson Street, New York, NY 10014.

Contents

Introduction

Like many of you, I've come to realize that reasonable taxes are probably a necessity in our great country. But I've also come to believe that the manner in which they're collected borders on insane. The fact that most financial planners, accountants, and even IRS agents continually come up with different answers to the same tax questions leaves me wondering how the average American has any prayer of getting it right.

So when I first heard about the FairTax proposal, which promises to radically revamp our tax system, I was filled with both hope and skepticism. That's because part of me is all for trying something new when the system is so broken. But there's also part of me that distrusts politicians and their ideas, especially one with such major implications.

To my great frustration, my search for answers about the FairTax proposal continuously put me in the path of one of two types of people—those who were adamantly for it and those who were passionately against it. In fact, either group was usually so pumped up on their viewpoint that they often made me feel like an idiot for not immediately jumping on the bandwagon or for expressing concern about their side's argument.

Well, this book is for the rest of the "idiots" like me—smart people who want to make an informed decision based on all the available information. In fact, you'll find that I avoid drawing a conclusion for you, unlike many of the other books you'll read about the FairTax. Rather, I'm simply going to look at the details of the FairTax proposal, what it might mean for both you and the country, and some "what if's" that neither side seems to want to deal with. Hopefully after reading this book, you'll feel empowered to have an educated conversation and make an educated decision.

In this book, you'll learn:

- What exactly the FairTax is and how it could dramatically improve our tax system.

- How exactly the FairTax is calculated and how it might compare to your current tax bill.

- Some of the major arguments made by both sides of the FairTax debate.

- How it might realistically affect the economy, government funding of programs, and the political process.

The Extras

Because there is so much to digest before you render a final decision on the FairTax, I've included some extras to help you in the process. You'll find these extras set aside in boxes throughout the book, with these easy-to-identify titles:

def•i•ni•tion

If you feel a little lost when your accountant starts throwing around the tax terms, you're not the only one. But have no fear! I've included nontechnical definitions of the most commonly used terms in each chapter.

To Be Fair

Since this book is all about showing you both sides of the argument, I've included numerous short counterpoints throughout the book. For a quick idea of how the other side of the argument would respond to an argument, give these a glance.

Your Wallet

While it's fun to talk theory, most people want to know how the FairTax and its different provisions would affect them. These snippets give you a quick breakdown of how different rules under the current and proposed systems affect your bottom line.

Look It Up

It's crucial with a proposal of this magnitude that you do your own homework. You're off to a great start by picking up this book, but you'd do yourself some good to spend some time with the outside resources mentioned in these sections.

Acknowledgments

As always, I'd like to thank my amazingly patient and wise editor at Penguin/Alpha Books, Mike Sanders.

To my agent, Bob Diforio at the D4EO Literary Agency. I'm continually thankful for your advice, mentoring, and hard work.

To the marketing and publicity gurus who have helped me make a career out of writing: Gardi Wilks and Patty Henek at Wilks Public Relations, and Dawn Werk at Penguin Books.

To my fellow writers at About.com, Investopedia. com, Helium.com, and elsewhere—thank you for your encouragement, wisdom, and support.

To all the folks at FairTax.org and the other grass-roots groups who have generously and patiently answered my questions.

To Dan Clark, Teri Rice, Laura Conrey, and the other tax experts I've known throughout my financial planning career—much of what is now commonsense for me was a question you answered at one point or another.

To my dad, Ken Clark Sr., who imparted to me the slightly masochistic view that doing your taxes is like solving a really fun puzzle.

To Drew, Price, and Ryan, whose adventures are more entertaining and satisfying than anything I could ever hope to write.

But most of all, as always, to my wife Michele. There's no doubt that being married to me has been "taxing." Your continued patience, love, and encouragement is a picture of who I hope to be someday!

Trademarks

All terms mentioned in this book that are known to be or are suspected of being trademarks or service marks have been appropriately capitalized. Alpha Books and Penguin Group (USA) Inc. cannot attest to the accuracy of this information. Use of a term in this book should not be regarded as affecting the validity of any trademark or service mark.

The FairTax Basics

In This Chapter

- Creating a national sales tax
- Basic arguments for the FairTax
- Basic arguments against the FairTax
- The history of the FairTax
- The need for tax and IRS reform

With the number of Americans advocating for a switch to the FairTax nearing one million people according to some organizations' estimates, it seems inevitable that a FairTax debate will eventually take center stage. Unfortunately, however, the FairTax suffers from a public relations problem in that some of its earliest and most visible supporters represented conservative politics. This, of course, has resulted in many on the left refusing to hear the potential merits of the FairTax plan.

Making matters more complex is the continued introduction of new legislation meant to ease the majority of Americans' annual tax burdens, leaving many correctly feeling as if something is currently being done to ease their tax burdens. There should be no surprise then that the FairTax, which creates a 23 percent tax on most Americans' spending, is less well received by people who do not fully understand it than ongoing proposals to simply lower the current tax rates.

In this chapter, we take a look at the FairTax in simple terms and the arguments for and against implementing it.

The FairTax in Simplest Terms

Though the title probably wouldn't be as catchy as "FairTax," this alternative plan for taxation could have more accurately been named the "SimpleTax." In reality and by comparison to the current tax system in the United States, the FairTax is amazingly simple. In a nutshell, it replaces virtually every existing federal tax (income, Social Security, gift, etc.) with one inclusive 23 percent sales tax that is paid at the retail level on new (not used) goods and services (everything from medical care to carpet cleaning). It does not tax goods or services that are purchased by businesses for business purposes, and it does not replace certain excise taxes, such as the federal gas tax.

In other words, the only tax you'd pay besides your state and local income and sales taxes is this 23 percent tax, collected when you purchase any new goods. Because of this, you'd no longer need to file an annual tax return, worry about saving receipts or proving deductions, or make life's most important decisions based on the tax consequences.

Your Wallet

According to TaxFoundation.org, the average American currently loses 28.2 percent of his wages to income taxes. This is on top of the 7.65 percent most people pay in Social Security and Medicare taxes. When the smoke clears, the average American is losing close to 35 percent of his income in taxes.

While this might lead some of you to immediately pick up the phone and call your senator, others of you may be shaking your head in disbelief at the idea of a 23 percent sales tax. But before you freak out about your already expensive life costing you 23 percent more, keep in mind what the FairTax would replace:

- A federal income tax that can range as high as 35 percent.
- Social Security and Medicare taxes (FICA or SECA) that cost both individuals and employers 7.65 percent on approximately the first $100,000 in each worker's wages (15.3 percent total).
- The *alternative minimum tax* (*AMT*) that ranges between 26 to 28 percent.
- A federal gift and estate tax that can range as high as 45 percent.
- Capital gains taxes (profits on the sale of investment assets) that range as high as 15 percent.

- Corporate income taxes that range as high as 38 percent.

def•i•ni•tion

The **alternative minimum tax (AMT)** is an alternative tax code already in existence, designed primarily to tax high-income Americans who otherwise go untaxed due to the use of certain tax deductions (for example, interest on a second mortgage) and exemption on certain types of income (for example, incentive stock options). Although it does not uniformly tax all high-income Americans, it does catch those whose income came from certain sources or utilized certain kinds of deductions.

In addition to eliminating all these taxes, it is argued that the FairTax would effectively eliminate the need for the IRS, tax preparers, and the annual stress of trying to understand and file a tax return. The elimination of all these would arguably save billions in both personal and government spending, as well as boosting people's productivity and moods around April 15th of every year.

The Quick Argument for the FairTax

The argument for the FairTax is a seductive one, honed over the last few decades by the people advocating it. In essence, it argues that switching to the FairTax system would accomplish five main things. The FairTax …

- **Makes taxation simple and transparent.**
  Under the FairTax proposal, everyone would
  know exactly what she's paying and when
  she's paying it. An individual could even go
  so far as to control the timing and amount of
  her taxation if she could control the timing
  and amount of her qualifying expenditures.

To Be Fair

Just to be clear, the FairTax is not a
"flat" tax, since it is neither calculated
on income nor is it technically flat (since
the FairTax is not calculated on all spending). It is a consumption tax, calculated
on what you spend on both services and
"new" goods.

- **Is revenue neutral or positive.** FairTax
  supporters argue that the FairTax is revenue
  neutral at worst, revenue positive at best. In
  other words, the FairTax plan will bring in
  the same amount of tax dollars or more without costing the average taxpayer anything
  more than he's paying already. We'll explore
  how this may be possible later in the book.

- **Will spur the economy.** One of the grand-
  est claims of FairTax proponents is that a
  national sales tax will spur the economy
  more than any single event in recent
  memory. This claim is in part based on
  the assumptions that the FairTax will keep

money from evaporating from businesses, attract foreign investments, effectively tax profits from illegal activities (as criminals get taxed when making purchases with their ill-gotten gains), and lead "offshore" money to return to the U.S. economy.

- **Eliminates taxes as a vote-buying mechanism.** One of the big arguments against the current tax system is that politicians can promise to give certain groups tax breaks while increasing the taxes on other groups to win votes. Since the FairTax theoretically taxes without prejudice on spending, politicians could no longer use this as leverage to gain votes.

- **Eliminates the IRS and tax preparation.** In establishing a simple method to calculate and collect a national sales tax, the FairTax effectively eliminates the need for the billions of dollars the government spends on the operations of the IRS (with over 100,000 employees) and Americans spend on their annual tax preparation.

The Quick Argument Against the FairTax

The FairTax is not without its vocal opponents, many of whom have understandably grown leery of politicians' tax promises. We'll also explore these arguments, some of which have merit.

- **The FairTax will raise costs.** At the center of this argument is the belief that the taxes currently *embedded* or included in the cost of everything we buy (from workers' payroll taxes to corporate income taxes) will not be eliminated from the price of goods, even though businesses no longer have to pay them. The overall effect is to actually increase the cost of living for many Americans.

def•i•ni•tion

An **embedded tax** refers to the concept that the cost of every good we buy is affected by the taxes that had to be paid to manufacture it. In other words, the higher the income taxes on the workers and the income and payroll taxes on their employer, the more our purchase is ultimately going to cost us.

- **The real rate is 30 percent.** One of the other main sticking points of FairTax opponents is that the real tax rate is not 23 percent, but 30 percent. As we'll look at in Chapter 2, both are simultaneously true, with the difference being hypothetically irrelevant.

- **The FairTax will cause job losses.** Opponents argue that the elimination of the IRS and the tax preparation industry will result in the loss of anywhere from 250,000 to 1,000,000 high-paying jobs nationwide.

- **The FairTax will result in underfunding.**
  Combining the mechanism for funding programs such as Social Security (FICA from your paycheck) into the same mechanism that collects all other sources of tax revenue will increase the risk that insufficient funds will be collected to pay for entitlement programs many Americans count on.

- **The FairTax creates windfalls.** By converting to the FairTax, many opponents point out that those who control much of the wealth in America will effectively dodge things like the accumulated capital gains on their investments and real estate, the estate tax, and other luxury taxes they have to pay.

- **The FairTax is a tax cut for the wealthy.**
  People arguing against the FairTax are quick to point out that someone who earns more than roughly $200,000 gets taxed at incremental rates starting at 28 percent and going as high as 35 percent. Further, more and more upper-middle-class Americans are now finding themselves subject to the alternative minimum tax, which taxes people at either 26 percent or 28 percent. Naturally, paying only 23 percent under the FairTax, only to the extent of what you actually spend, might seem like the upper classes are getting a tax break.

The History of the FairTax

How far the FairTax has come in the couple decades since it was first pondered is simultaneously amazing and not surprising. In large part, it is the result of a 700,000-person-strong grassroots movement that sprang from a three-man think tank. However, its popularity has definitely been aided by the cheerleading of some high-profile media personalities and a *New York Times* best-seller—something we should always remember when looking at this from both sides.

The Founders of the FairTax

The origins for the FairTax were simple enough. In the mid-1990s, a group of wealthy Texas businessmen committed $4.5 million of their resources to help fund research into designing a better tax system. As the story goes, they had no one alternative system in mind; rather, their research was driven by the recognition that the current system seemed broken. Another $17 million, raised from various sources, augmented this seed money, and all of it was thrown at the problem of revamping the tax system to make it more equitable and less burdensome to every American taxpayer.

To Be Fair

The FairTax may be a grassroots campaign, but it's definitely roped in its fair share of high-profile supporters, such as presidential candidate Mike Huckabee, action star Chuck Norris, syndicated talk show host Neil Boortz, and "famous for being famous" Joe the Plumber.

The research that was conducted included both grants made to respected researchers and tax experts from schools like Harvard, MIT, Boston University, University of Maryland, and Rice University, and grants given to think tanks such as the National Bureau of Economic Research and the Baker Institute for Public Policy. This research was on top of numerous surveys conducted among various demographic groups that included everyone from CEOs to mailroom clerks.

By 1999, the results of these studies had grabbed the attention of U.S. Representative John Linder (R-GA) and laid the groundwork for a bill in the House of Representatives entitled "The Fair Tax of 1999," or "H.R. 2525." The bill, now known just as H.R. 25, was highly touted for its bipartisan authorship and support, even though it actually included only one Democrat—Collin Peterson (Minnesota). Though the bill drew support from 56 congressmen and women, it failed to gain enough support to go before a vote.

Since then, Congressman Linder has reintroduced the bill each congressional cycle, garnering an increasing level of support but still failing to reach the voting stage. Senator Saxby Chambliss (R-GA) has introduced a parallel senate bill, known as "S 296," which has met with only moderate success and has not proceeded past the committee stage.

Whether or not you agree with the FairTax, one of its most impressive features has been the grassroots movement that surrounds it. Led by the Americans for Fair Taxation (AFFT), this group and talk-radio hosts like Neal Boortz have spearheaded rallies that claim to have attracted tens of thousands of people in various cities around the country. Even political pop star Joe the Plumber has managed to get in on the act, pitching the FairTax on paid TV commercials.

The FairTax's Underlying Argument

While there is a very wide variety of beliefs about who should be taxed, how much they should be taxed, and how those tax dollars should be spent, one thing seems undeniable—the current tax system is out of control. In my 10-plus years as a financial planner, I can tell you from experience that 99.9 percent of people don't know as much as I do about taxes, and I'm still utterly confused at times. This includes a long list of both accountants and IRS agents, who incorrectly and inconsistently explain certain aspects of the Internal Revenue Code. Filing your taxes has become the equivalent of showing up to your high school calculus final and realizing that none of the stuff you studied is on the exam.

Many Americans live in fear (an unfounded one, I believe) of the IRS, the audit process, and the ensuing penalties. They spend huge amounts of time and money to take away the mystery and danger from the tax-filing process, while also making decisions based solely on the tax consequences as opposed to what is truly the right choice for them, their family, or their business. Their desks are overwhelmed with records and receipts, their financial lives are confusing to the point of rendering many financially illiterate, and their paychecks have been whittled away by myriad payroll taxes that most can't even begin to explain.

> **To Be Fair**
>
> Many of the FairTax supporters portray the IRS as a cash-hungry organization full of agents who love to torture innocent taxpayers through unfair audits. In reality, the IRS historically audits less than 1 percent of taxpayers making under $100,000 per year. Further, with the IRS having a limited amount of resources to perform audits, those who are audited are carefully selected based on the likelihood of a major error or tax cheating having occurred. The IRS does not have the time or resources to simply go fishing in the average family's tax return.

Then again, many Americans don't live in fear because they manipulate their tax returns or even avoid the tax system altogether. Whether the system became so complex that it forces people to cheat on their tax returns or people cheat on their tax returns because it's human nature, the reality is the same—millions of people abuse the tax code each year, costing the government over $300 billion! Add in the fact that hardcore criminals such as drug dealers aren't likely to file tax returns on their millions in profits, and the amount of uncollected taxes rises to over a half a trillion dollars! The existing tax system and the over-stretched IRS are not equipped to catch the majority of these people, leaving the rest of us to shoulder an unfair tax burden.

To Be Fair

Although most Americans are generally displeased with the U.S. tax system, their opinions continue to grow slightly more favorable each year. According to a 2009 Gallup poll, 61 percent of Americans believe the amount of tax they currently pay is fair. The poll also showed a sharp decrease in the number of people who believe they are paying too much, as well as an increase in the percentage that believe that lower-income Americans are pulling their weight.

In an effort to understand many people's zeal to reform the current tax system (both inside and outside the FairTax movement), consider these additional facts, which we'll explore later:

- According to the National Society of Accountants, the average cost of getting a tax return prepared hovers around $200 annually. This can easily climb into the thousands for small business owners.

- According to the nonprofit Tax Foundation, total "compliance" costs of all taxpayers is now over $250 billion per year, including both dollars spent and lost productivity.

- The IRS budget for 2008 exceeded $11 billion!
- A recent estimate by *USA Today* put the U.S. tax code and supporting publications at over 67,000 pages!

The Least You Need to Know

- The FairTax is a 23 percent national sales tax on services and the purchase of new goods that would replace virtually every existing federal tax, including income taxes.
- FairTax fans believe it will be a much fairer and simpler way to collect the same amount (or more) of tax revenue, while simultaneously spurring the economy.
- FairTax opponents believe the program favors the rich, who have untaxed accumulated wealth, while displacing hundreds of thousands of jobs and raising consumer prices.
- A simplified tax system, be it the FairTax or another alternative, would likely save the government and taxpayers billions of dollars annually in tax compliance costs.
- While the FairTax movement is spearheaded by some visible figures and loud voices, it is equally driven by hundreds of thousands of fed-up Americans.

2

FairTax Myths and Misunderstandings

In This Chapter

- Where the FairTax didn't come from
- The real costs of the FairTax
- It's probably not a magical economic cure
- The possibility of both a FairTax and an income tax

FairTax lore and legend has taken on a life of its own, with its perceived strengths and weaknesses becoming far more grandiose than what would likely occur in reality. In fact, depending on who you talk to, the FairTax is either going to save America or sink it. Rarely do you hear someone say something along the lines of, "Yeah, I think it's an interesting plan with some kinks that need to be ironed out." Maybe I'm the first.

Whether it's people's passion getting the better of them or a lack of understanding leading to an unfounded hope or fear, many people I talk to don't quite seem to understand what they're saying. Or if they do, they see it in such black-and-white terms that there can be no other possible outcome besides what they envision. In your evaluation of the FairTax, you must put some space between yourself and both of these points of view. As we evaluate something as radical as changing our country's tax system, brutal honesty and logic grounded in reality are crucial to making the right decisions.

I'm not going to pretend that I have all the answers, but I can guarantee you that the "absolutes" you'll find in this chapter aren't absolutes. The FairTax, in all its novelty and with all its potential, is not a cure-all for our country's problem. Nor as countries with relatively similar (though not identical) *value-added tax (VAT)* systems prove, the FairTax will not cause the apocalypse.

def•i•ni•tion

A **value-added tax (VAT)** is a type of sales tax. With VAT, each merchant or manufacturer essentially pays tax on the value they add to a product. For example, if raw materials cost a manufacturer $10 and they sell it to a merchant for $20, the manufacturer would collect and pay tax on the $10 in value they added.

Myths About the Origins of the FairTax

While the origins of the FairTax have little if any bearing on whether or not its theories and assumptions are sound, many treat them as if they do. With the help of the Internet, those for and against have listened to and continue to spin some pretty tall tales about its origins.

For openers, let's just rattle off the easy list of who was *not* involved with the creation of the FairTax proposal:

- Any U.S. president (including the current one)
- Neil Boortz, Hugh Hewitt, Mike Huckabee, Chuck Norris, or any other media personality
- George Soros, Warren Buffet, Bill Gates, or any other well-known billionaires we love to hate
- The Communist or Socialist parties
- The U.S. Chamber of Commerce or the Small Business Administration

Beyond these, which I hear tossed around only occasionally, a few other FairTax birthplaces are worth dispelling in detail. These are the ones I hear touted more frequently, whether in Internet chat rooms or on either side of the lines at the relatively new "Tea Party" movement.

Look It Up

Perhaps the best account of the FairTax's origins are in Neil Boortz and Rep. John Linder's original FairTax book entitled, *The FairTax Book: Saying Goodbye to the Income Tax and the IRS.*

Antitax Groups

The FairTax movement, much to its dismay, often gets lumped in with the antitax movement. These folks, often called "tax protesters," believe all taxes are unconstitutional and should be abolished completely. Many of them refuse to file tax returns, claiming they are exempt under Section 861 of the tax code—a strategy that often results in jail time. Over the years, some of these tax protestors have actually engaged in violent activities, such as planning to bomb IRS facilities.

Sadly, media coverage of the Tea Party movement that started in 2009 captures a fairly eclectic mix of people on film. It's not uncommon to see handwritten signs right next to each other that say "FairTax Now" and "Down With Taxes." Of course, that's a confusing and conflicting message for many who have never heard of the FairTax, leading them to believe the FairTax means "no tax."

Although some "tax protesters" may see the FairTax as a better option than the current system, that's as far as the two movements overlap. Most FairTax supporters are moms, dads, students, professionals, and blue-collar workers who simply have a major issue with the state of our current system. They recognize that taxes are a necessary evil in our society and seek to replace the current system with a better one—the same mindset as the three original Texas businessmen who set about trying to research a better alternative.

Bipartisan Roots

One misunderstanding perpetuated by some FairTax supporters, which borders on a half-truth in my opinion, is that the FairTax was bipartisan in its roots. That would be a truly attention-grabbing fact if it were true, but the numbers themselves don't exactly look bipartisan, as most of us envision the term.

While I'm sure some plain old citizens from both parties have believed in the FairTax from its inception, there's a huge imbalance historically in where congressional and senate support comes from. In fact, of the 54 members of the House of Representatives that originally supported the bill in 1999, only 1 was a Democrat. Of the three senators who supported the parallel bill in the Senate, none were Democrats. A decade later, at the time of this book's writing, the number of congressional and senate Democrats officially onboard with the FairTax has not changed—still just one.

To Be Fair

From the FairTax's first legislative introduction in 1999 up through mid-2009, President Barack Obama has remained silent on the matter, expressing no opinions for or against the FairTax. His staff, however, has been fully briefed by the staff of the Americans for Fair Taxation organization.

So, if we're arguing technicalities, I guess you could say that the FairTax had bipartisan support. In reality, though, Republicans at the top levels of government almost exclusively support the bill, with one Democrat tagging along. That's not to say that others don't whisper support in Washington's corridors of power. But when push comes to shove, they still refuse to put their names on it after more than a decade since its initial introduction.

Scientologists

While you might think it's a joke that I've taken a whole section in this book to dispel the notion that Scientologists helped birth the FairTax, it's for real. In fact, a good number of people who oppose the FairTax still throw this one in as icing on their cake of opposition. So with all judgment withheld on Scientology as a belief set, let me say unequivocally that the Scientologists had nothing to do with the FairTax's creation. Again, that doesn't necessarily mean there aren't Scientologists who support it, but they were not its authors.

The confusion comes from the fact that a prominent Church of Scientology member founded a similar group called the Citizens for an Alternative Tax System (CATS) nearly a decade before the first FairTax bill was circulated. In both design and leadership, the two organizations and their plans showed noticeable differences that would not be easily confused by anyone following the tax reform movement.

Myths About the FairTax's Costs

If you jump into a FairTax debate anywhere, no doubt a discussion of what the FairTax will actually end up costing people will consume the majority of it. FairTax supporters argue that it will cost Americans nothing more than they pay now, possibly even lowering their cost of goods while simultaneously increasing their spending power. FairTax opponents predict spiraling costs on everything from the cost of a latté to the purchase of your dream home. The reality, like most things, probably falls somewhere in between.

Your Wallet

If you're dying to get a quick picture of what the FairTax is going to mean for your household, FairTax comparison calculators are available online at places like FairTax.org.

Everything Will Cost 23 Percent More

Perhaps the most basic misunderstanding and myth about the FairTax is that everything will cost 23 percent more than it already does. If this has crossed your mind, don't feel dumb. After all, it is a 23 percent sales tax, right?

If the FairTax was simply added to our current tax system without other taxes being removed, it very likely would result in everything costing 23 percent more than it currently does. But remember, the FairTax actually replaces most existing federal taxes.

And the removal of these other taxes, especially corporate income taxes and payroll taxes, will play a crucial role in your cost of living not skyrocketing. These so-called "embedded taxes," which raise a company's overall cost of doing business, would cause a company's profit margin to instantly climb when removed. And while these companies may be tempted to keep that increased profit instead of passing it on in savings to their customers, most items in most markets will be subject to competition that will squeeze some or all of this profit back out.

Imagine that your local potato grower sells a bag of potatoes for $10. According to research funded by the Americans for Fair Taxation, these potatoes have $2.20 of embedded taxes in them, which would be removed under the FairTax.

While it might be tempting for the potato grower to charge his usual $10 per bag plus the new 23 percent FairTax, this pricing scheme probably won't last long. In fact, in probably just a matter of days, a price war would erupt, and another potato grower down the street would begin selling his potatoes for $9 in an attempt to steal some business. Heck, even at $9 per bag, he's still making more money because his embedded taxes are gone, too.

But it won't take long for the first farmer to undercut the second to stabilize his own market share and even try to grab a bit of the other guy's. In fact, this would likely go back and forth until the price of a bag of potatoes dropped back to a price where the farmers were making the same profit as before the FairTax, somewhere around $7.80 a bag. Of course, once the FairTax is added back to this, it would put those potatoes right back at $10.

As a side note, you may have noticed that $7.80 plus 23 percent tax doesn't actually equal $10. Rather, it equals only $9.59. That's because you've just calculated the FairTax on an *exclusive* basis (or $7.80 plus 23 percent). In reality, the proposed FairTax is computed on an *inclusive* basis, which means that the price of the item already includes the 23 percent tax, which would actually have to be right around $10 to ensure the farmer still earns the same amount. We'll talk more about this in a second.

def•i•ni•tion

In its most basic definition, an **inclusive sales tax** is one that is included in the price of the item you buy, while an **exclusive sales tax** is added to the price of the item.

In the end, customers will likely pay the same or less than what they're already paying for most of their purchases, even after the FairTax is added in. But as we'll also look at more later in this chapter, such a price drop depends on economic principles that FairTax supporters can't guarantee, such as pure competition, the availability of substitute goods, and a lack of coordination or collusion between sellers.

Everything Will Cost 30 Percent More

FairTax critics are quick to point out that the FairTax is computed on an inclusive basis, instead of an exclusive basis. They'll tell you that when you look at the FairTax on an exclusive tax basis, the real tax rate is actually 30 percent. Sadly, both sides spend a lot of time nit-picking this argument, when the overall reality is that prices should hypothetically stay the same on most goods. Ultimately, if prices remain the same and sufficient taxes are collected out of that amount, there's not much room for complaints.

To Be Fair

Comparisons between the inclusive FairTax rate, an inclusive income tax system, and exclusive sales taxes ultimately fail because it's like comparing apples to oranges. To get a real picture of what the FairTax means for you, avoid getting caught up in semantics about the rates. You should really base your decision on the change in cash in and out of your unique household that the FairTax causes.

The best way to understand the difference between tax inclusivity and tax exclusivity is to examine the way you usually pay sales tax and then to realize that the FairTax does it differently.

Under most sales tax models, the tax is simply added to the price of your purchase. Many of us come to understand this reality sometime during our childhood when we've saved our money for that big purchase and gone to the toy store, only to be told the $20 toy actually costs $21.50 with tax. When this happened, the tax we experienced was "exclusive" or "above and beyond" the price the retailer showed on the item, which is the way most sales taxes currently function.

Let's say, however, you're now all grown up and take your niece to the store to make her first big purchase. She picks out a toy with a price of $20, takes it to the register, and the clerk announces that she owes $20 even. Naturally being a little confused, you ask the sales clerk if he forgot to include sales tax and are told that the store's new policy *includes* the sales tax in the price. You smile, leaving happy that your niece seemingly got a deal.

But what that ultimately means is that the price for the toy really wasn't $20 but was effectively something lower with sales tax built into the final price. In this case, you're now dealing with an inclusive sales tax system, similar to how the FairTax would function.

Under the FairTax, a business owner who needs to sell a toy for $20 to cover his costs and make his target level of profit would actually end up pricing the item for $26 to cover for the FairTax. When 23 percent for the FairTax is removed from the sales price of $26, it leaves the owner with net revenue of $20.02, very close to the $20 target he had hoped for on the item.

Of course, that's where it gets confusing, because adding $6 to the price of a $20 item is really a 30 percent increase. But when that $6 is removed from the $26 as taxes, leaving the owner with roughly $20, it now only represents a 23 percent tax on $26. In short, an owner must increase his pricing by 30 percent to account for the later removal of the 23 percent FairTax. Do you feel like you just drank a Slurpee too fast?

Before you agree, but also challenge that this is exactly what the critics were worried about, you've got to realize that the toy store owner, who no longer suffers from embedded taxes, will have likely lowered his price significantly before adding 30 percent to cover the later removal of the 23 percent FairTax.

Look It Up

To truly understand the pro-FairTax position on embedded taxes and their effects on prices, review Harvard economist Dan Jorgensen's research, which was funded by the Americans for Fair Taxation.

Based on studies quoted by the FairTax supporters, the taxes currently embedded in all goods, including our $20 toy, are 22 percent of their retail cost. That means that of the toy store owner's $20 price, $4.40 represents embedded taxes. Hence, if these embedded taxes were removed, the storeowner could charge $15.60 and make the same profit as when he was previously charging $20.

So, if this $15.60 price is then increased by 30 percent to cover the later removal of the FairTax, the item now costs $20.28, nearly what it did before. When the 23 percent FairTax is eventually subtracted from that amount and sent to Uncle Sam, the owner is left with $15.61, roughly a penny more than he needed to hit the embedded-tax free revenue target of $15.60.

Granted, the consumer in this example is paying 28¢ more than he was under the old system, or a 1.5 percent increase. But remember, he is no longer paying income tax, FICA, etc., which for most Americans greatly exceeds the 1.5 percent increase in price. That's far from the 30 percent increase, relative to current prices, that FairTax critics are claiming we'll all experience.

Everything Will Cost the Same

So far, we've attempted to shed some light on the idea that everything will cost 23 percent or 30 percent more than it already does. In reality, most prices should drop significantly before being increased by 30 percent to allow for removal of a 23 percent inclusive FairTax—all of which yields roughly the same price for the consumer who theoretically has more money to spend.

But I don't want you for a second to think I'm jumping on board with the FairTax supporters who think all prices on all items will drop in the same manner. In fact, basic economic theory tells me this perfectly balanced price drop and subsequent increase works only if a number of factors exist. If these factors fail to exist, then the price drop may be much smaller (even nonexistent), resulting in an overall price increase to the consumer. Remember, the FairTax does not force businesses to lower their costs but rather counts on market forces to do that.

Unless a business owner is feeling very patriotic or very fair, it's unlikely that he'd immediately lower his prices by the amount of any embedded taxes that are removed from his cost. In the case of our farmer, this competition would come from other local farmers selling their goods at lower prices, starting a bidding war for the customers' business. But what if there aren't any other local farmers?

Look It Up

For one of the clearest overviews of basic economic principles including competition, substitution, and price collusion, check out Tom Gorman's *The Complete Idiot's Guide to Economics.*

For example, I love driving the majestic Pacific Coast Highway between San Luis Obispo and Carmel in California. In fact, the only thing that has a shot at ruining the ocean views are the two or three gas stations spaced out along the 150-mile drive. These gas stations, which are the only game in town, can charge whatever the heck they want for gas, and they know it. To a large degree, under the FairTax they'd have no competitors to force them to drive down their prices to match the embedded taxes they no longer pay.

While FairTax supporters would point to studies that say otherwise, the reality is that when just a few companies control a large amount of the market share for a product, they can easily work together to keep prices artificially high so they all benefit. If you don't think this can happen, just look at the oil and diamond cartels like OPEC or DeBeers that actively work to keep prices at a level they can live with. If in our previous example, the three gas stations on the Pacific Coast Highway got together and agreed to lower their prices by only 10 percent instead of the 22 percent expected under the FairTax, the rest of us couldn't do much about it.

For competition to drive down prices under the FairTax or any other system, the goods a competitor is offering must be similar enough that consumers are willing to accept them as a substitute. While this may not be a problem with tomatoes or toilet paper, it definitely may be an issue with brand-name goods that consumers accept no substitute for.

For example, many people feel that an iPod is the only way to go when buying an MP3 player. While other companies may make similar items, for many there is just no substitute for an Apple. Because of this, brands like Nintendo, Mercedes, and Chanel have more room to capture that excess profit without driving off customers. Sure, some may bolt for another brand, but there's no telling whether or not these brands will find a happy equilibrium, where a higher price and fewer customers are more profitable than lowering their price by the 22 percent of embedded taxes that have been removed from their costs.

The FairTax Is Too Expensive to Implement

While it's an easy myth to dispel, the idea that the FairTax is too costly or difficult to implement is worth addressing since it comes up over and over again. In reality, the FairTax would be extremely easy to implement for most larger retail establishments who use computer-based registers that a small number of manufacturers distribute and maintain. In these cases, switching over would be as simple as a one-time software update and a repricing of the items in their stores. It's likely that most retailers could accomplish both of these over a weekend.

To Be Fair

In any discussion about the difficulties in implementing the FairTax, keep in mind the incredible amount of time and money spent on tax compliance under our current system. If the FairTax were to be implemented, any first-year headaches would likely be overshadowed by later gains in efficiency.

Easing this transition is the fact that all businesses that collect the FairTax will receive a .25 percent slice of the pie for their duties, paid out of the over-all FairTax revenues collected. Since most of these businesses already collect state and local sales taxes, they'd essentially start getting paid for something they're already doing. Not a bad deal for most businesses, since it will probably cost them less than they'll earn.

Myths About the FairTax Benefit

Early in my career, during a major burnout stage, I wanted to do anything but deal with the chaotic stock market on a daily basis. The phone calls from panicked clients during the end of the dot-com bubble left me dreaming of an easier existence. One day, driving past the local strip mall, I saw a vacant retail space. In that moment, I had a flash of brilliance—"*I'll open a restaurant!* That'll make life so much easier!"

Naturally, when I penciled it out on paper, everything worked. I would make the same or more money, work the same or less hours, and not have to worry about anything besides keeping people's glasses full of whatever they're drinking. Sadly (or perhaps brilliantly), my wife encouraged me to get some outside counsel on the idea. Upon investigation, I learned that most restaurant owners worked twice as hard, made half as much, and were stressed out like no other. In hindsight, I can easily see that my disgust for my current situation made me over-confident in the "what-ifs" of a potential change.

With this in mind, continue to look into the qualifications of those who pound the table the hardest for the FairTax. Do they have a background in economics, finance, investing, taxes, or retail pricing? Or is their only real background a well-founded disgust with the way things are? If it's the latter, double-check the facts they're using to support the FairTax against the opinions of academics and other professionals. When you do, you'll often find that these well-meaning individuals are neither completely wrong nor completely right in their assumptions about the "guaranteed" benefits of the FairTax.

The FairTax Will Supercharge the Economy

While we delve more into the actual economic effects of the FairTax in Chapter 6, it's worth clarifying here that the predictions of FairTax fans are simply that—predictions. Although there is a definite possibility that the FairTax could put a spring in the economy's step, the estimates that it would lead to an overnight financial boom seem a tad far-fetched.

Don't get me wrong—I and many others hope they're right. I hope businesses will expand. I hope foreign money will be attracted to the United States. I hope more money will find its way into the stock and real estate markets, etc. But I also truly believe that anyone, regardless of his or her background, who thinks he can predict the outcome of one variable's effect on an economy such as ours has either greatly oversimplified the math or greatly overestimated his ability. We need look no further than the recent economic meltdown to realize that these economists, financiers, and politicians are, at best, making educated guesses like everyone else.

The reality is that any broad economic gain hoped for under the FairTax could just as easily be offset by something having nothing to do with it. Stock prices, real estate values, employment figures, overall GDP, etc., can be affected in both the short and long term by everything from terrorist attacks to the meltdown of just a single key company like AIG. That's not to say that the FairTax won't be a net positive to the economy, but we simply have no way to truly know.

No More Taxes

The idea of just a single, predictable tax sounds fairly close to the American dream, but it's not what the FairTax is promising. Thus when you hear someone say that the FairTax replaces every other tax you currently pay, they're just downright misleading you.

I'll spare you the rehashing of what taxes the FairTax does replace (see Chapter 1) but will tell you what taxes it *doesn't* replace:

- The federal gas tax
- *Excise taxes* on alcohol, tobacco, and other items
- State and local income taxes
- State and local sales taxes

- State and local hotel and rental taxes
- State luxury taxes on high-price items
- Taxes paid to foreign governments

def•i•ni•tion

An **excise tax**, sometimes referred to as a *sin tax* when it's on items such as alcohol or tobacco, is a tax used to essentially penalize certain industries that are thought to cost society more than others. For example, more and more states are raising their tobacco taxes to fund health-care systems that must care for smokers.

Easy Transition

While it wouldn't be that hard for most businesses to retool their pricing and point of sales systems for the FairTax, that doesn't mean it'd be an easy transition for the rest of us. Specifically, the passage of FairTax legislation could actually result in a situation where people are charged both the FairTax and an income tax at the same time. You read that right—because of the design of the FairTax bill, it's possible (though not probable) that you could be paying your normal income tax plus a 23 percent sales tax.

For the FairTax to truly be effective and remove the open-ended possibility that a politician might reintroduce an income tax at a later date, we'd need to repeal the Sixteenth Amendment. For this to happen, two thirds of the House of Representatives and the Senate would need to vote in favor, followed by three quarters of the states. If this doesn't happen, the FairTax could continue to exist alongside the government's right to levy personal income taxes.

> ### Look It Up
>
> The Sixteenth Amendment to the U.S. Constitution gives the government the right to levy taxes without apportioning it among the states based on population. It's the basis for our federal income tax based solely on income.

Thus, getting the FairTax adopted by the House and Senate is the easy part, but gets us only halfway to a new tax system. Erasing the permanent possibility of the income tax requires a whole separate action, which could be affected by simple Beltway politics. In the end, it's possible the FairTax would get "sunseted" a few years into its existence, requiring the nation to re-embrace the current system, including a rebuilding of the dismantled IRS. Surprisingly, many FairTax supporters have never heard about this possibility, because if they had, they might be a tad more cautious about jumping on the bandwagon.

The Least You Need to Know

- The FairTax was started by a group of Houston businessmen and has received far more support from Republicans than Democrats.

- In a best-case scenario, the removal of embedded taxation and the addition of a FairTax leaves the prices on goods and services right where they were prior to the FairTax.

- Higher overall prices may occur where there is a lack of competition or with items that consumers are unwilling to accept substitutes for.

- Though the FairTax will likely contribute some to the economy, there is no real way to predict a sharp increase in GDP or wealth due to the complexity of the economy.

- A transition to the FairTax could hypothetically create a situation where individuals would be charged both an income tax and the FairTax.

Chapter 3

The Math of the FairTax

In This Chapter

- Determining the FairTax rate
- Goods and services subject to tax
- Who would owe the FairTax?
- FairTax collection procedures

Thankfully, calculating the FairTax is a whole lot less painful than high school trigonometry and doesn't require an advanced calculator with graphing abilities.

In fact, simplicity has always been one of the supposed hallmarks of the FairTax system. By simplifying the tax calculation and removing the ridiculously complex system of deductions and credits, even the most math-phobic folks can understand what they're going to pay and when. Even better, with some simple planning, they'll arguably have greater control over what they pay and the timing.

The Basic FairTax Formula

As mentioned in previous chapters, the FairTax is a 23 percent national sales tax on purchases of new items. And while on the surface, that lives up to the promise of being ridiculously simple, there's still a little more (but not a whole lot) to it than that.

> ## Look It Up
>
> When it comes to the actual wording of the FairTax rate, every American should read it for themselves instead of taking my, or anyone else's, word for it. You can find the short passage describing the rate by using the hyperlinks at FairTaxGuide.com.

According to the actual FairTax legislation, the tax rate during the first year of the FairTax's existence would be 23 percent. But after that first year, it would revert to a "floating" rate comprised of three separate components. These components combine to form what is collectively known as the *combined federal tax rate percentage*.

def•i•ni•tion

> The **combined federal tax rate percentage** is the actual term for the FairTax tax rate and is comprised of three separate rates— the general revenue rate, the OASDI rate, and the hospital insurance rate.

The combination of these three rates is quite simple to understand but also illustrates the very real possibility that the FairTax percentage can change due to fluctuations in just one of these underlying rates.

- **The general revenue rate**—This rate, currently set at 14.91 percent, serves as the primary replacement for the income taxes you currently pay.

- **The OASDI rate**—The term OASDI stands for "old-age, survivors, and disability insurance" and is part of what you currently associate with FICA (Social Security) taxes. Currently, this rate is set at 6.2 percent for employees (which the employer also matches for a total of 12.4 percent), but is expected to total 6.31 percent in the first year of the FairTax. This 6.31 percent collected in the first year of the FairTax is meant to replace the combination of the employer and employee contributions currently contributed.

- **The hospital insurance rate**—More commonly known as the "Medicare deduction" on your paycheck, this rate represents the current cost of ensuring that every American has his or her emergency medical needs met in retirement. Currently, this rate is set at 1.45 percent for employees (which the employer also matches for a total of 1.45 percent) but is expected to total 1.78 percent in the first year of the FairTax. Like the OASDI rate, this 1.78 percent collected in the first year of the FairTax is

meant to replace the combination of the
employer and employee contributions currently contributed.

Calculations and Changes to the Three Rates

One of the most common misconceptions about
the FairTax is that the rate would permanently be
set in stone or that it would take a majority vote in
Congress to raise the rates. While this is true with
regard to the general revenue rate (14.91 percent),
it is not necessarily true of the OASDI or hospital
insurance rates. In fact, the FairTax legislation
contains provisions that require these numbers to
be automatically adjusted annually in response to a
preset formula.

Under Section 904 of H.R. 25 (The FairTax Act of
2009), the OASDI and hospital insurance rates shall
be calculated to yield the same amount of revenue
that the government would have received if payroll
taxes were still collected under the prior tax system.
This means that the rates added to FairTax's general
revenue rate of 14.91 percent must yield the same
revenue as the 12.4 percent and 2.9 percent currently collected for OASDI and hospital insurance
respectively. But, theoretically, since the amount
of taxable transactions the FairTax is calculated
on is much greater than the amount of wages that
payroll taxes are currently calculated on, OASDI

and hospital insurance rates included in the overall FairTax rate should go down significantly.

In other words, whatever amount is needed to match what would have been collected for OASDI and Medicare under our current system must be added to the FairTax's 14.91 percent general revenue rate in every year after the FairTax's first year in existence. If a 5 percent tax is required to cover Social Security and Medicare costs, the overall FairTax would be 19.91 percent (14.91 plus 5 percent). However, if a 10 percent national sales tax is required to cover these amounts, the actual FairTax rate would be 24.91 percent (14.91 plus 10 percent). To make a long story short, after its first year, the actual FairTax rate could be more or less than 23 percent.

To Be Fair

In all fairness, we must acknowledge that the Social Security system is dramatically underfunded at this point. If something is not done to increase revenue and/or decrease costs, the system is headed for bankruptcy. Whether it is our current payroll tax rate or the rates calculated under the FairTax plan, a rate increase is a very real possibility. FairTax proponents are simply arguing that this increase will be far more likely under our current system than under the FairTax system.

Goods and Services Subject to the FairTax

Few things incite as much concern and confusion as what goods and services the FairTax would actually be calculated on. But it's within these rules that the FairTax's authors have perhaps made the most progress in creating a tax system that is truly fair (i.e., doesn't favor certain industries or classes of people), though it still seems to favor business owners slightly.

As you read through the explanations of what is and isn't taxable under the FairTax system, remember the goal is to tax things only once at the consumer level. Goods and services purchased in the course of business are not taxed until they are actually sold to the consumer or used for nonbusiness purposes.

New Versus Used

The biggest line in the sand when it comes to what the FairTax is applied to is "new" versus "used" goods. Specifically, the FairTax applies only to transactions for new items, with items meeting the definition of "used" being exempt from taxation. The FairTax defines "used" as anything that has previously had the FairTax paid on it at a retail level, as well as property owned prior to the date that the FairTax legislation takes effect. So, technically, a car that has never been driven (making it essentially new) would be considered used if it had been purchased by a consumer prior to the FairTax being enacted. It would also be considered used if it had been purchased after the FairTax had been

enacted but another consumer had already paid the
FairTax on it once before.

Additions to the FairTax

To many people's chagrin, the FairTax will be levied
on a number of things that have escaped taxation
since the creation of the personal income tax. But
that's not to say life will ultimately cost more than
it does now. Most fans of the FairTax would argue
that the increase to one's take-home pay under the
FairTax would more than cover the addition of
taxes to these items. Let's hope they're right!

- **All services**—Probably the most surprising
  potential for change under the FairTax
  would be the taxation of service industries
  not currently taxed. This would include
  everything from legal fees to medical bills to
  commissions on trading stocks. No industries are exempt as long as their services
  are purchased for nonbusiness purposes. In
  other words, a lawyer who sells his services
  to both businesses and individuals would
  collect a tax on the individual consumer but
  not the businesses, since it is a necessary
  business expense.

- **Leases, rental agreements, and loans**—
  Whether you're leasing or buying a car,
  renting an apartment, or financing a home,
  you'd likely pay the FairTax on some or all
  of your monthly payment. The exception
  would involve purchasing a used home or
  vehicle, in which case the FairTax would be

charged only on the interest portion of your monthly payment, not the principal amount.

- **Household employees**—Thanks to a number of high-profile "Nanny Tax" scandals in recent years, most Americans are aware that hiring domestic help requires an individual to pay some taxes to cover the cost of his employee's Social Security and Medicare (7.65 percent) plus any required unemployment taxes. Under the FairTax, household employers (known officially as "taxable employers") would have to pay the government a 23 percent FairTax on wages paid to such employees.

- **Gambling**—While many Americans could care less about the taxation of gambling and gaming, a certain portion of America enjoys weekends away in America's neon meccas and Native American casinos. So the idea that the casinos (not the gamblers directly) would be forced to pay the FairTax on their profits may sound a little scary to casual card sharks and slot players. While the full ramifications of this—like casinos changing their odds, payouts, or comps—is not fully known, it is important to keep some perspective and realize that the profits of many casinos are already taxed under the current system.

- **Travel**—The FairTax would be applied to most travel costs, including airline tickets, car rentals, and hotel stays.

- **Utilities**—All utilities would also now be taxed at the FairTax rate. Although some argue that the removal of embedded taxes and increased paychecks would offset this taxation, others are quick to point out that many utilities (especially tax-free municipal utilities) have very little embedded taxes in the first place.

Your Wallet

Interestingly enough, the FairTax legislation as it is currently written taxes only 50 percent of travel costs outside of the United States. Thus, if all other costs remain the same, a $5,000 vacation to Disney World will result in more FairTax being charged than a $5,000 vacation to France.

Other Exemptions from the FairTax

In addition to used items not being taxed, a number of transactions may also be exempt from the FairTax. Depending on how the FairTax collection process is actually structured, a consumer may claim an exemption at the time of the transaction or claim a credit on his tax filings. Some exemptions include the following:

- **Investments**—Although the FairTax is assessed on the cost of investment services, it is not levied on the investments themselves. For example, if a retiree invests $100,000 with a financial advisor and pays a $2,500 commission, the $100,000 does not get taxed but the $2,500 does.

To Be Fair

Many FairTax advocates incorrectly state that there is no deduction available for college tuition under the current tax code, when in fact there is. Although the laws may change after this book is printed, there are both sizeable tax deductions and tax credits for college tuition under our current tax laws.

- **Education expenses**—Thankfully, the already out-of-control costs of education would not be taxed under the FairTax. Whether it is college tuition or private elementary school, no FairTax would be added to these amounts.

- **The Business Use Conversion Credit**—This credit allows a business owner to recoup some or all of the FairTax paid on personal property that he later uses for his business. For example, if you bought a computer for personal use but later decided to use it at your business, you may get a credit that erases part of the FairTax you previously paid for it.

- **The Export Sales Credit**—This credit allows a business owner to reduce the FairTax paid on items destined for export and sale outside of the United States.

- **The Administration Credit**—This credit helps business owners cover some of their

costs in collecting the FairTax and preparing
the required monthly reports. Because this
credit awards the business owner the greater
of $200 or .25 percent of the tax he collects
per month, some fear it represents a hand-
out to small business owners that can easily
exceed their costs in collecting the FairTax,
preparing the paperwork, and mailing a
check.

- **The Bad Debt Credit**—If an individual or
  a business experiences a loss because of a bad
  debt (e.g., someone doesn't pay him back the
  money he is owed), he may claim a FairTax
  credit roughly 30 percent of the amount of
  his loss.

- **The Insurance Proceeds Credit**—This
  credit allows an individual who receives a
  payout from any kind of insurance contract
  to recoup some or all of the FairTax paid
  on purchases made with those proceeds.
  This essentially makes insurance benefits
  income tax–free, just as they currently are.
  For example, under the current tax system,
  someone receiving a $100,000 payout from
  a life insurance policy would not pay any
  income tax on that. But under the FairTax,
  they'd pay sales tax on whatever they spent
  the $100,000 on. That's where this credit
  comes in: by allowing someone to avoid the
  FairTax on the $100,000 of purchases, it
  essentially keeps insurance benefits tax-free.

Who Pays the FairTax?

One thing that makes the FairTax unique is who it hypothetically taxes. Unlike the current tax system, whose bite some can avoid both illegally and legally, the FairTax system catches virtually everyone in its web. And while it hopefully doesn't end up costing the average taxpayer any more than it already does, it does promise to create revenue from those who've otherwise dodged the taxman.

The Government Itself

Under the FairTax proposal, Uncle Sam (and your local county and state) gets taxed just like everyone else—the only difference being that you spend less on jet fighters and office supplies than they do. Of course, just like any other business, if the government is an intermediary purchaser (not the end consumer), no tax is charged in lieu of the eventual end consumer paying it.

Tax Cheats

As is mentioned elsewhere in this book, an astounding number of Americans lie on their tax returns, hide income, inflate deductions, etc. Sadly, this lays an even greater tax burden on the rest of us who choose the more expensive route of honesty. But the FairTax promises to change all of that.

Because the FairTax is a simple sales tax collected at the time of purchase, tax cheats and dodgers would have their bag of tricks largely taken away from them. Since the vast majority of America's spending dollars flow through a relatively small number of mega-corporations (Wal-Mart, Exxon Mobil, etc.), they'd have no real way to dodge paying taxes on most day-to-day purchases. Every time they'd buy a gallon of gas or a quart of milk, these individuals would be forced to pull their economic weight.

While some "resourceful" Americans would try to find ways to skirt the system, the vast majority of businesses big and small wouldn't play ball because the chances of getting caught for tax evasion would be greater than ever. Between the policing of state sales tax revenues (something we've effectively done for years), the FairTax's provisions that reward people who anonymously turn in dishonest businesses, and the relatively small size of most day-to-day transactions, the incentives for dishonesty just don't outweigh the gains.

Criminals

Famous Chicago gangster Al Capone was eventually jailed on, of all possible charges, tax evasion. Part of what eventually led to his prosecution was the realization that his lavish lifestyle didn't match up with his failure to claim any taxable income over a number of years.

Unlike the Americans with legitimate income and expenses who lie about these amounts on their tax returns, a small number of Americans engage in illegal activities and have no intention of ever acknowledging these "businesses" on their tax returns. Naturally, this *shadow economy* represents

a huge amount of income that goes unaudited and
untaxed because its presence is simply unknown.

def•i•ni•tion

> The **shadow economy** refers to the under-
> ground or illegal economy that surrounds
> illicit activities ranging from drug trafficking
> to illegal gambling. Most of the money
> "earned" in this economy avoids taxation,
> something the FairTax hopes to fix.

While the FairTax doesn't put these criminals out
of business, it does ensure that at least some of the
money they make from these operations gets taxed.
Just like those who choose to misrepresent their
legal income and deductions, those who engage in
illegal activities also buy gas, candy bars, and holiday presents at the mall. When they do, they'll pay
the FairTax on the fruits of their illegal labors.

Legal and Illegal Aliens

While there's no doubt that most foreign citizens
who come to this country (be it legally or illegally)
are not evil or criminally minded people, many
would argue they receive more from the system
than they pay into it. Whether it is health care,
emergency services, or welfare programs, many feel
that these individuals receive government benefits
while simultaneously being paid under the table
with no income or payroll taxes withheld. Even for
legal nonresident aliens, many argue that no income

tax revenue is generated because it is paid when they file taxes in their home country.

Under the FairTax, the contribution of these individuals to the economic system would now be indisputable. Just like others who have escaped taxation for other reasons, aliens residing in the United States would pay into the system every time they purchase goods and services. Many argue this would help stem the tide of illegal immigration, since these individuals would be clearly paying a substantial tax into a system from which they may not eventually benefit.

International Tourists

There's no doubt that the United States is one of the must-see destinations for the rest of the world. No matter where they travel from, global tourists flock here to not just see but also buy pieces of America's icons. They don't just go home with pictures, but with suitcases full of blue jeans, tennis shoes, electronics, and "I Love New York" T-shirts.

In addition, international tourists pump billions of dollars into local economies by staying at hotels, renting cars, eating at restaurants, and taking in the sights. Under the FairTax, every dollar spent on these items would be subject to the FairTax, hypothetically pumping additional funds into the economy. Of course, as we'll see in Chapter 6, many are rightfully concerned that increasing the cost of a visit to America by 23 percent would cut down on tourism.

The *De Minimis* Rules

One of the most common questions people ask when they learn about the FairTax is something along the lines of, "My daughter occasionally babysits; is she supposed to collect the FairTax from the people she babysits for?"

Naturally, expecting a 16-year-old to collect the FairTax on her $5-per-hour babysitting gig, file the appropriate paperwork, and remit it to the appropriate taxing authority seems a bit of a stretch. The good news is that the FairTax proposal authors agree.

Similar to the current tax laws, the FairTax proposal allows for people to earn a certain amount of money before they must collect the FairTax. Under the current legislation, the *de minimis* dollar level is $1,200 in "occasional or casual sales." According to FairTax supporters, this would include things like teenage babysitters and occasional eBay sellers. In a similar fashion, the FairTax legislation also allows purchasers of $400 or less in goods imported into the United States for personal (not business) use to avoid FairTax liability.

def•i•ni•tion

The **de minimis** rules in both the current tax code and under the proposed FairTax set certain dollar minimums under which no tax is assessed. The term *de minimis* comes from Latin, meaning "of a minimum amount."

Interestingly enough, a somewhat random *de minimis* exception is stuck into the FairTax proposal for financial intermediaries (real estate brokers, financial advisors, lenders, etc.). In what seems to be a bit of a subsidy to the financial industry, the *de minimis* amount is not the standard $1,200 but $10,000. In other words, if a self-employed financial intermediary generates $10,000 or less in receipts per year, the money won't be subject to the FairTax.

Collecting the FairTax

For the most part, collection of income taxes currently happens in two places. First, deductions are made from workers' paychecks each pay period, or in the case of a self-employed worker, submitted quarterly to the IRS. In both instances, these are merely estimates of what the employee is likely to owe come April 15th. Second, around April 15th, taxpayers file their returns and pay any additional taxes they owe.

Those who work in a payroll department, as well as anyone who's ever filed a tax return, can tell you these activities take an immense amount of time and effort under our current system. By comparison, collection of the FairTax generally happens in three easy steps, involving far fewer people in the process.

First, under the FairTax, a seller of goods or services collects the estimated 23 percent tax at the point of purchase. Depending on the amount of tax the seller collects annually, he may need to deposit the tax collected for each Friday-to-Friday period into a separate dedicated account within three business days of the end of the week.

Second, the seller must submit these amounts collected at the business level to the collecting state or agency by the 15th of the month for the calendar month that just ended. In other words, all businesses must submit January's collections to their state by February 15th.

Lastly, the administering states have five days to turn over any money they receive (less the state's .25 percent for collecting it) to the U.S. Treasury. States and businesses failing to submit collected funds in a timely manner can be penalized by adding interest to the amount due.

The States' Role in Collection

The basic premise behind the collection of the FairTax is that individual states are the most capable and experienced parties when it comes to collecting a national sales tax. In fact, almost every state currently collects some type of sales tax.

Considering that these structures are already in place, it's arguable that states will have little additional cost in collecting a national sales tax. The .25 percent they receive to collect the tax would easily offset any actual cost. According to the FairTax legislation, states that are unwilling or unable to collect the FairTax can contract out to other states or the federal government to handle the collection.

The most obvious benefit of handing off the responsibility for FairTax collection is that it eliminates the need for a massive federal agency such as the IRS. This, in turn, saves billions annually in collection costs and government spending, allowing this money to be funneled back into other government programs or even to be cut from the budget altogether.

Extensions and Refunds

No two tax terms are more familiar to Americans than "extension" and "refund." Perhaps that's because we're a nation of procrastinators and overspenders who can always use a little extra time and money. So it goes without saying that many are concerned about whether these concepts will make their way into the FairTax.

First, let's look at the coveted (and misunderstood) tax refund. Under the current tax system, many people count themselves lucky if they get money back on April 15th. They feel like it's free money and they just won the lottery. Of course, many fail to realize they are simply getting the amount they overpaid out of their paycheck throughout the year, which ultimately represented an interest-free loan to Uncle Sam.

Under the FairTax system, we'd have far fewer refunds than we have now. That's not because most Americans would be taxed more, but because they paid only the tax they owed at the time they purchased something. The only reason the amount due would get reduced and they'd get a refund in the classical sense is because they could claim one of the credits mentioned at the beginning of this chapter (a rare occurrence). That's not to say we wouldn't be getting money from the government—in fact, it's just the opposite. Under the FairTax, every man, woman, and child would get a monthly check known as the "prebate," something very different than a refund (more on that in Chapter 4).

Your Wallet

The FairTax legislation requires that any refunds be made within 60 days of filing the appropriate paperwork.

For business owners who collect taxes, as well as those rare individuals required to submit the FairTax on their own or are able to claim a refund, the government will offer extensions. But just like extensions under the current system, these are extensions to file, not to pay, the tax due. Under both systems, a person can request an extension of time to turn in the supporting paperwork, but he still must pay any tax due by the normal deadline.

Under the FairTax, people required to file a tax report or return for the previous month are granted an automatic 30-day extension by filing a standard piece of paperwork. If they need more time, they can request an additional 30- to 60-day extension, which the FairTax proposal instructs the states to "grant liberally."

Audits, Penalties, and Records

Despite what some FairTax supporters are saying, audits would still exist under the FairTax proposal.

But the vast majority would focus on businesses, with the state that oversees collection primarily determining the selection instead of the federal government. Those individual taxpayers who find themselves in an audit would likely be those who made questionable use of one of the few FairTax credits on their purchases.

According to the FairTax proposal, the "burden of production" of records falls on the taxpayer or business. This means that the taxpayer or business has a responsibility to provide valid records documenting his FairTax calculations, collections, and use of credits. To fully meet this requirement, taxpayers and businesses must keep their records on file for six to seven years, depending on the type of information.

The actual "burden of persuasion" falls on the tax-collecting authority (the state or federal government) conducting the audit. That means that once the taxpayer has produced the documents, the government must prove him guilty, instead of the taxpayer proving himself innocent.

Some of the civil and criminal penalties for breaking various rules (noncompliance) under the FairTax are as follows:

- **Late remittance of reports or taxes—** Taking too long to submit your FairTax paperwork can result in a monthly penalty of .50 percent per month of the amount owed, up to 12 percent. Late submission of money owed can result in an additional 1 percent per month, up to 24 percent.

- **Failure to collect tax**—A business owner failing to collect the tax from customers can face penalties ranging from the greater of 20 percent of the uncollected amount or $500 and/or up to one year in jail.

- **Claiming a false exemption**—Individuals or businesses claiming a fake exemption or credit from the FairTax can also be slapped with the greater of 20 percent of the uncollected amount or $500 and/or up to one year in jail.

- **Failure to remit collected taxes**—Those business owners who collect the tax but keep it for themselves can face a fine that is the greater of 50 percent of the collected amount or $1,000, plus up to two years in jail.

The Least You Need to Know

- The actual FairTax rate may vary due to changes in one of the three underlying base rates.

- Previously untaxed services—such as medical care, legal advice, rent, commissions, and loans—will not be subject to taxation.

- Used goods, costs related to a business, educational expenses, and the value of investments made will not be taxed.

- Businesses and states act as the primary collectors of the FairTax, submitting their collected monies once per month.

- Though audits and penalties would still exist under the FairTax, far fewer Americans will find themselves sitting across from an IRS agent.

4

The FairTax and Your Wallet

In This Chapter

- The FairTax "pay raise"
- Calculating your monthly prebate
- Stocks, bonds, and the FairTax
- Real estate in a FairTax nation
- The FairTax and interest rates

If the FairTax lives or dies based on one thing, it'll be how the average American perceives its effect on his or her wallet. While the politicians may have an indispensable role in the FairTax becoming law, undoubtedly a public outcry will push it one way or another. As many have come to realize, most politicians relish their jobs far more than they relish the right piece of legislation and fear the angry mob far more than they fear the downfall of America.

Naturally, the favorite weapon on both sides of the FairTax argument is how the FairTax would affect your wallet versus the current system. People are quick to forecast that the FairTax will either bring prosperity or ruin to America's pocketbooks, although few actually recognize the true complexity of the matter. Ironically, the net effect would most likely be somewhere in the middle, with few dramatic changes to individual American's personal finances.

Money In, Money Out

For most Americans, the first question will always be, "Does the FairTax leave me with more money or less?" The answer, as we previously touched on in Chapter 2, is virtually impossible to pin down because there is just no way to predict whether market forces will cause the cost of goods to fall enough to erase the addition of the FairTax. Further, the effect of the FairTax on everyone's take-home pay will not be uniform—some people will take home much more, while others will see no real change in their take-home pay.

In other words, there is no way to truly predict whether the price of a compact disc or a loaf of bread will drop enough, due to the removal of embedded taxes and the addition of market forces, to fully absorb the addition of the FairTax. Further, if these items actually increase in cost, the ability of Americans to afford them out of their paychecks will not be the same across the entire population.

The Cost of Living

Since we touched on it at length in Chapter 2, I'll spare you the full rundown again. But, in a nut-shell, the fans of the FairTax claim the prices on everything will virtually stay the same under the FairTax. Even though we would be adding a 23 per-cent inclusive sales tax to the item (which actually seems to raise the price 30 percent), they believe that most business's costs of goods would also drop by this amount or more thanks to the removal of embedded taxes. Because of the drop in the costs of goods (which initially generates more profit) and the subsequent price war between businesses, this short-term increase in prices will be squeezed out and prices will return to where they started.

Look It Up

The number one source for pro-FairTax estimates about how the economy would perform under the proposed system is FairTax.org. On this website, you can find dozens of "white papers" that tout the expected economic benefits of the FairTax.

This assumes the presence of competition, goods, and services that consumers are willing to accept as substitutes and the absence of collusion (businesses working together to fix prices). Since no one can guarantee these things, especially in the early days of the FairTax, some prices will likely be higher than they are now. This will be especially true in more rural areas, on unique and brand-name products, and on services that don't have embedded costs in them. Over time, some costs will ultimately remain the same; some will slowly drop; some will experience a moderate increase; and some will experience a permanent increase close to the amount of the FairTax.

Americans' Paychecks After the FairTax

If the idea of a 23 percent national sales tax is the biggest turnoff to the FairTax proposal, the idea of a larger paycheck is no doubt the biggest turn-on. In fact, the increase in take-home pay is perhaps the largest single benefit touted by FairTax supporters. Heck, there's even a pro-FairTax book whose title touts the FairTax as a "25 percent raise!"

Viewing the FairTax as "a raise" is more than a tad misleading since a national sales tax may offset some or all of that; nonetheless, it's true that Americans' paychecks will be larger. How much larger is a much different matter, and the effects will vary dramatically depending on each household's income level. That's because the increase comes from the fact that income taxes and certain employment taxes are no longer removed from your paycheck.

Your Wallet

If you currently get money back every April 15th, you don't need to wait for the FairTax to increase your monthly paycheck. Visit your accountant or the IRS's withholding calculator, and submit a revised W-4 to your employer's payroll department. By doing this, that money will stay in your paycheck each month instead of the government holding on to it until tax time.

Under the FairTax, the tax withholding system, which essentially collects a "down payment" toward what we owe on April 15th, would disappear. In other words, since we'd no longer have a personal income tax, there'd be no need to take any money out of our paycheck for it. For some Americans, especially high-income people, this would represent a huge change in their monthly cash flow. However, for Americans who have little or no withholding taken from their paychecks because they ultimately owe little or no taxes each year, the effect would be negligible.

In addition to feeling the pinch of federal income tax withholding, most Americans have also come to loathe the FICA deductions from their paychecks. This represents another 7.65 percent (6.2 percent for Social Security, plus 1.45 percent for Medicare) that evaporates from most peoples' paycheck. Since virtually every American, including the lowest-income earners, must pay this, its elimination would effectively boost monthly paychecks by this amount. Don't forget, however, that roughly one third of the FairTax's rate is meant to replace what is no longer collected from workers' paychecks, so we're not really getting off scot-free.

Of course, FICA taxes are twice as painful for self-employed individuals and small business own-ers since the government requires an employer to match his employees' FICA contributions (actually called SECA when one is self-employed). That means, for someone who is effectively both her own employer and employee, she's on the hook for 15.3 percent or a little less after deductions. For these folks, the creation of the FairTax may leave them feeling like they won the lottery. Not only would their paychecks increase anywhere from 10 to 35 percent because income taxes would no longer exist, but they'd also increase another 15 percent because FICA (or SECA) would no longer exist either. That could easily equate to a 25 to 50 percent bump in monthly cash flow for self-employed earning Americans. Even better, they'd go from having their Social Security and Medicare contributions costing them double what other Americans pay to paying the same as everyone else because of the FairTax's nondiscriminatory structure.

Your Wallet

Many people don't realize the Social Security portion (6.2 percent) of their payroll taxes is capped at a certain dollar amount. For example, the maximum wage per taxpayer that this withholding can be calculated on is $106,800 for 2009; wages earned above that amount escape the Social Security tax. However, the Medicare tax (1.45 percent) is charged on all earnings without limit. Under the FairTax, there is no limit on the amount paid into either system by any one taxpayer.

A World Without April 15th

I'd be remiss if we didn't discuss how the death of our annual tax-filing day (April 15th) would affect American pocketbooks. For most people, filing their taxes is either a win or a lose, with very few ties. That is, most people either get money back, which they incorrectly view as a win, or end up owing money and feeling like they yet again lost their battle against the IRS. Very few Americans, in fact, pay exactly what they owe throughout the year in their payroll deductions and end up owing or being refunded nothing.

Under the FairTax, for those people who perpetually owe money every year, the dark day of April 15th would become a thing of the past. For people who regularly get money back, however, it might feel like someone cancelled a national holiday. Many of these people, in poor financial style, blow their refund on something frivolous since it is a "freebie" from Uncle Sam. They sadly fail to realize the government is simply returning their excess "down payment" against what they were expected to owe. For these people, the FairTax wouldn't result in a true loss, as much as the death of a financial delusion.

One group truly would have good reason to mourn the loss of April 15th—certain lower-income taxpayers over age 25 who have been eligible for the *Earned Income Credit*. The EIC, as it is more commonly called, is actually a direct government subsidy paid to lower-income earners, even if they owe no federal income taxes.

Take, for example, a single parent raising two children on an income of $20,000 per year. She likely owes no federal income taxes whatsoever *and* receives over $4,200 from the government under the EIC. For these folks, the FairTax will sting mightily, even in spite of the "prebate" they'd receive under the FairTax (more on this in a bit).

def•i•ni•tion

> The **Earned Income Credit** (EIC) is a form of government welfare currently paid to qualifying households that make roughly $42,000 or less for a married couple ($39,000 if single). The EIC may either be distributed as part of someone's tax refund or as part of his or her regular paycheck.

The Loss of the Mortgage Interest Deduction

While many Americans don't have the foggiest idea how their taxes are actually calculated under the current system, the vast majority can tell you that having a mortgage will land you a major deduction. It's this deduction, or rather the potential loss of it, that worries many Americans and has the majority of an industry (real estate agents) running scared.

Many fear that without the home mortgage interest deduction, much less the FairTax being added to many people's monthly payments, homeownership would become unaffordable for most Americans. Generally though, this would not be the case under the FairTax, since the deduction doesn't save most Americans as much as they think, as well as the fact that most people's take-home pay will rise due to the absence of withholding and payroll taxes.

First, let's examine the fallacy about the value of the mortgage interest deduction under the current system. Most Americans do not realize that if they do not itemize their annual deductions (including the mortgage interest deduction), they still receive a standard (blanket) deduction that saves them a substantial sum of money. Further, because someone loses the standard deduction if she chooses to list out each deduction one by one (called "itemizing"), owning a home may not lower her taxable income much more than if she were a renter.

For example, a married couple can claim a standard deduction of $11,400 for the 2009 tax year, or they can list out each of their deductibles and hope that they save more. Thus, if their only "itemizable" deduction is the $1,000 in mortgage interest they pay each month ($12,000 for the year), they're deducting only $600 more ($12,000 – $11,400) than they did prior to owning a home. This slight difference in deductions only saves them a total of $100 to $200 at tax time based on their tax bracket, compared to being a renter.

The Estate, Gift, and Alternative Minimum Taxes

Average folks from all over the political spectrum most detest the parts of the income tax code that include the estate, gift, and alternative minimum taxes (AMT). These taxes ensure that people who have otherwise played by the rules are taxed again and again. Needless to say, higher-income

Americans—who are often victims of the AMT, a tax designed to snag many higher-income earners that would otherwise legally escape taxation—wouldn't mind seeing the current system die. Likewise, families with at least $1 to $2 million in net worth—who often get pummeled by estate and gift taxes if they give away or die with too much money—would also be happy to see the FairTax eliminate these laws.

> **To Be Fair**
>
> While some might point out that the FairTax benefits the wealthy, it's important to note that the loss of the mortgage interest deduction costs those in the highest income tax brackets the most. As far as actual dollars, the elimination of a $1,000 monthly mortgage interest deduction for someone in the highest bracket (35 percent in 2009) would cost them $250 more per month than someone in the lowest bracket.

For the minority of Americans who are hit by these, especially the estate and gift taxes, the effect on their wallet is traumatic to say the least. Simply by dying or giving too much of their wealth away in any one year, they can rack up taxes close to 50 percent and even more if the assets are held in tax-deferred accounts like IRAs or 401(k)s. Further, many family-owned small businesses, especially those with much of their net worth tied up in assets such as real estate or machinery, are often torn apart at the seams when they're hit with a large estate tax bill just because one of the owners dies. The net result of the FairTax is that much more money would stay put in the highest-earning and wealthiest of families.

The Prebate

In an effort to keep the FairTax from placing a disproportionate burden on lower-income individuals and families, its designers created the Family Consumption Allowance, better known as the *prebate*. This monthly subsidy from the government is meant to offset the FairTax charged on the most basic of living expenses. In the spirit of being fair, the FairTax's authors would award the prebate to everyone, from the poorest to the wealthiest. Bill Gates would get the prebate right along side someone scraping along at minimum wage.

def•i•ni•tion

> The **prebate** is a monthly advance given to consumers to cover the cost of the FairTax on all expenses up to the National Poverty Guideline. In other words, every American would have a certain portion of his spending, based on family size, escape the FairTax.

Naturally, when people first hear about the "prebate" offered under the FairTax plan, they may be prone to think of the famous warning from Homer's *Iliad* about the Trojan Horse—"beware of Greeks bearing gifts." That's because the idea of the U.S. government, which many have viewed as their financial arch-enemy, sending everyone money each month seems a little too good to be true.

Well, it's true. Of course, we can't forget that the prebate is offered under the FairTax system, which does tax every end-consumer roughly 23 percent on the purchase of his goods and services. This naturally leads some FairTax opponents to cry foul, claiming that the advocates are trying to push this plan through with a distracting wave of cash in front of voters' faces.

How the Prebate Is Calculated

The calculation of the prebate is both simple and automatic. In other words, the government automatically determines the amount for each qualifying person or family. You don't need to be good at math beyond counting the number of people who live in your household. You simply fill out a form, submit it to the government, and they do the rest.

But for those of you who like crunching the numbers, the methodology is simple enough. First, determine the annual poverty level for a family of your size. You can find this information on the website for the Department of Health and Human Services at aspe.hhs.gov/poverty.

After identifying the annual poverty level for a family of your size, divide it by 12 to determine your monthly poverty level. Then, simply multiply this amount by the current year's FairTax rate, and that is your prebate amount.

For example, at the time of writing this book, a single father raising two kids (regardless of his income) would receive a monthly prebate of $350.94, calculated as follows:

1. The 2009 annual poverty guideline for a family of three is $18,310.

2. Divide $18,310 by 12 to arrive at the monthly poverty guideline ($18,301 ÷ 12 = $1,525.83).

3. Multiply the monthly poverty guideline of $1,525.83 by 23 percent to determine your monthly prebate, which would be $350.94 ($1,525.83 × 23 percent = $350.94).

If you are married, you get a slight boost in the monthly amount the FairTax is calculated on to help eliminate the "marriage penalty" that exists in the poverty guidelines. Under the current system, the poverty guideline for two single adults in a domestic partnership is much higher than for a married couple, something that the authors of the FairTax sought to fix.

To illustrate this, let's slightly change the preceding example. It's still a family of three, but instead of a single father with two children, it's a married couple with one child.

Your Wallet

If you live in Hawaii or Alaska, the federal poverty guidelines are roughly 20 to 30 percent higher, which means that residents of these states will also receive a prebate 20 to 30 percent larger than the rest of the country.

1. Calculate the marriage penalty by computing the difference in annual poverty levels for a family of two and two individuals ($21,660 – $14,570 = $7,090). You need to complete this first step based on two people regardless of the actual size of your family, because you're trying to calculate the value of the "marriage penalty." The amount you calculate in this step will be added to whatever your family would have received anyway.

2. Look up the 2009 annual poverty guideline for our family of three ($18,310).

3. Add the annual poverty guideline for a family of three to the marriage penalty amount ($18,310 + $7,090 = $25,400).

4. Divide the new combined amount by 12 to arrive at the adjusted monthly poverty guideline ($25,400 ÷ 12 = $2,116.67).

5. Multiply the adjusted monthly poverty guideline by 23 percent to determine your monthly prebate, which would be $486.83 ($2,116.67 × 23 percent = $486.83).

Who Gets the Prebate?

You might argue that the prebate may be the part of the FairTax system most prone to abuse, but that doesn't necessarily mean it is a faulted system, since the same type of problem currently exists with people claiming false exemptions on their tax return or receiving a deceased person's Social Security checks. Thus, in an effort to ensure that everyone entitled to a prebate gets one and those that aren't do not, the FairTax's authors have put a number of specific rules into place.

- **Annual registration**—The head of each household must file an annual registration that includes his name and Social Security number, as well as that of his spouse and any legally dependent children.

- **Excludable individuals**—Incarcerated individuals and noncitizens may not be counted as part of a household or claim a prebate.

Look It Up

The FairTax legislation sets out harsh penalties for people filing fraudulent prebate registrations. According to Section 504 of Title III of the FairTax, convictions can bring a fine of $500 or 50 percent of the false rebate amount (which ever is greater), plus up to one year in jail.

- **College students**—If someone receives over 50 percent of his financial support from a household and is a student at least five months during the calendar year, he can still be claimed as part of a registered household.

- **Children and custody agreements**—If there is split custody of a child due to a divorce or separation, the parent with 50 percent or more custody is entitled to claim the child, unless the other parent has relinquished that right in writing.

Delivery of the Prebate

Some critics have rightly brought up the fact that delivering millions of monthly prebate checks is a major task. While it no doubt is, also realize that a check would not be mailed to every American— just one check per household. It is also likely that many Americans would opt for direct deposit or a rechargeable debit card (similar to the current food stamps program), both of which the FairTax permits.

Nonetheless, it is still a monumental undertaking, especially considering the FairTax Act requires mailing the checks or releasing the money by the first of each month. But compared to the current costs and man-hours involved in running the IRS, distributing the prebate would seem like a relative walk in the park.

The Social Security Administration, which is already distributing funds monthly on a smaller scale to the nation's retirees, would handle the actual distribution of the prebate.

Your Investments Under the FairTax

If any one country has redefined the word "retirement," it's America. After a lifetime of work, the typical American may dream of some mix of relaxing, traveling the world, mastering his hobbies, and even starting a new business. But like all American dreams, most people have realized that no one is going to achieve it for them. Naturally, this leaves many Americans, especially those in or near retirement, wondering what will happen to their nest eggs under the FairTax.

To Be Fair

FairTax advocates argue that the U.S. investment markets, already the premier destination for the world's investing dollars, would strengthen under their plan. Realistically, though, further investment in the U.S. markets always has been and always will be affected by a number of factors beyond the direct effect of U.S. income tax policy, such as the dollar's value, the creditworthiness of the United States, and the emergence of competing markets across the globe.

Stock and Bond Prices

While some FairTax fans believe the plan would send the prices of stocks to new heights, this seems highly unlikely. If the FairTax is ultimately revenue neutral (collects the same amount of money) as its authors promise, there really would be no more money in the broad economic system to create demand for stocks and drive up the prices. Further, since the FairTax fans argue that competitive markets would drive out the gain that's experienced when embedded taxes are removed, corporate profits would likely remain about the same.

To Be Fair

Some FairTax fans argue that stock prices are simply based on the present value of their future expected cash flows. And since they expect future cash flows to increase under the FairTax, they also expect stock prices to increase. Unfortunately, the market is nowhere as rational as the simple models used to theoretically value stocks, with bubbles and crashes defying even the most trusted quantitative models.

While some would also argue that the removal of taxes on investment income would help spur new investment in the stock markets, it's just as likely to put some downward pressure on stock prices. That's because the earnings on bonds and other interest-paying instruments, which were previously taxed at a higher rate than long-term stock gains, will now be tax-free the same as stock gains under the FairTax. This makes bonds even more competitive with the stock market on an after-tax basis and history has shown that, as this gap between the riskier stock market and the less risky investment-grade bond market tightens, money actually flows out of stocks and into bonds. That actually provides an increased incentive, especially during lousy markets, for people to sell their stocks (which pushes down prices) and buy bonds.

That doesn't mean all bonds would be affected the same. In fact, the bond market itself may go through some internal upheaval with regard to prices and yields as certain bonds that were previously tax-favored lose this status, namely *municipal bonds*.

def•i•ni•tion

Municipal bonds are bonds issued by state, county, and city governments and agencies to help pay for public works. To encourage investors to buy these bonds, the federal government does not generally tax investors on the interest they earn. This gives people an incentive to buy these bonds compared to other types of investments, especially bonds issued by corporations.

Under the current system, municipal bonds are exempt from federal income tax, which allows them to pay a lower yield (costing state and local governments less in interest), while still offering a competitive after-tax return compared to corporate bonds. With the FairTax's elimination of tax on the interest earned on corporate bonds, their rates would likely fall some, while municipal bond rates would climb. This stems from the fact that many investors will rush toward corporate bonds for the now significantly higher yield, driving up the price, which actually pushes their yield back down. Simultaneous with this, existing municipal bonds would actually have to raise their yields (by lowering their prices) in order to become competitive again.

In summary, the FairTax is most likely to have two effects on stock and bond prices:

- Stock prices will stay about the same or drop slightly in the short term but will still provide the highest return over extended periods of time.

- Corporate bond yields will drop and municipal bond yields will climb. Municipal bond holders who choose to get rid of their bonds before they mature will probably show a loss, while corporate bond holders will probably show a gain if they sell before maturity.

Tax-Deferred Accounts Under the FairTax

The FairTax plan would affect tax-deferred accounts, such as 401(k)s, IRAs, and Section 529 College Savings Plans in two primary ways. First and foremost, these accounts would no longer be subject to taxation when the money is withdrawn.

For people who've contributed money to a classic
401(k), IRA, or other deductible account, this would
mean that they'd effectively avoid ever paying
income tax on that money. Naturally, potentially
saving hundreds of thousands of dollars endears
the wealthiest of these account holders toward the
FairTax.

Your Wallet

It may not be a bad thing if the FairTax
brings an end to the company-sponsored
retirement plan as we know it. The reality
is that these plans often come with higher
expenses and limited investment choices
compared to individual investments outside
these accounts. Under the FairTax, where
investors have no tax incentive to invest
through their employers, many investors
would be able to invest their money more
efficiently with better investment selection.

For individuals who had contributed to a nondeductible account, such as a Roth IRA or a Section
529 plan, this means they'd be able to withdraw
the money for nonqualified purposes (other than
for retirement or paying for college) and avoid
the taxation that would have occurred as well. No
official word has been given yet on what would
happen to the 10 percent penalty currently assessed
on early or nonqualified withdrawals, but with the
elimination of the IRS, it's likely that this would be
eliminated, too.

The second effect of the FairTax on these accounts is their eventual death as we know them. Since investment earnings are not taxed under the FairTax, there'd be no need to put long-term savings into accounts meant to shelter them from taxes. While employers would almost certainly continue to provide employee savings plans similar to 401(k)s, it is hard to imagine anyone using them unless the company offered a matching contribution.

The elimination of taxation on tax-deferred accounts, as well as the need for these accounts, would likely have no substantial overall effect on the value of stocks and bonds. While some people who currently invest in their employer 401(k)s may cease to invest if their company doesn't offer one, it's expected that most people who are prone to save and invest will continue to do so elsewhere.

Real Estate Prices

The overall effect on stock and bond prices is somewhat predictable because of the sheer size and liquidity of those investment markets. Money and assets change hands almost instantaneously and are not subject to things like geographical differences in pricing, local economies, and credit availability. But these factors make the effect of the FairTax on real estate prices much harder to predict.

Like stock and bond prices, consumer demand drives real estate values. But unlike the stock market where a lack of consumer demand may simply result in a lower price, a lack of demand in real estate means the inability to sell your home at a price sufficient to cover your mortgage balance. For example, it was not uncommon in the most recent real estate downturn to see severely discounted homes *still* sitting on the market for 6 to 12 months, if not longer. In other words, the real estate market can be highly *illiquid*, which means that predicting the FairTax's effects on it is next to impossible.

def•i•ni•tion

Illiquidity refers to the ability of the owner of an asset to quickly convert that asset into cash without having to severely lower the price. For example, $100,000 in gold coins is much more liquid than a $100,000 painting.

What we can predict is that there would initially be a gap between the cost of new and used homes. Remember, all used goods (those owned prior to the FairTax and those on which the FairTax has been paid at least once) no longer get hit with the FairTax. That means that in any given neighborhood, a home built immediately after the FairTax is enacted may be selling for 0 to 23 percent more (depending on how much embedded tax gets removed) than a home built and sold right before the FairTax.

While FairTax fans would tell you that those prices would equalize (the price of used homes would rise and new homes would fall, until they're roughly the same), a stagnant real estate market may prove them very wrong. Since homes are not identical (no two houses have the same view, the same carpet, the same wear and tear, etc.), a house whose price is only slightly higher under the FairTax may be unsellable on a street with non-FairTax houses also for sale. You don't have to look any further than homebuyers' intentional avoidance of homes subject to Mello-Roos (higher property taxes on certain newer developments) to recognize that this is at least a possibility.

All this is not to say that the FairTax is not the right choice for tax reform. Rather, it is to say that with certain illiquid and nonidentical investments (two slightly different houses), there is no guarantee of immediate, or even permanent, price stability under the FairTax.

Loan Interest Rates Under the FairTax

One of the biggest oversimplifications under the FairTax proposal is the assertion that interest rates will immediately drop 25 percent or more. Part of this oversimplification comes from the failure to mentally separate how the extension of credit works on an individual versus an institutional (corporate or municipal) level. In reality, large corporations that borrow money by issuing bonds have a much easier time raising money than someone trying to get a mortgage for a house. The corporations' borrowing rates are driven by the analysts' ratings of those companies and the hunger of investors for certain types of bonds.

To Be Fair

Anyone who believes he can neatly sum up the effects of a tax system on interest rates (or the economy, for that fact) in a few hundred pages, much less a few paragraphs, is oversimplifying things. Whether you are for or against the FairTax, you should realize that the greatest economic minds of our time struggle to make heads or tails out of these complex scenarios.

Individuals shopping for interest rates, on the other hand, are at the mercy of a number of unique factors, including the government's willingness to subsidize consumer lending through organizations like Fannie Mae (home loans) and Sallie Mae (student loans), the lenders that are reasonably available to them, and the type of loans they're seeking. Further, the rates offered by lenders to individuals can be substantially affected by that corporation's financial stability, whereas there is much steadier demand for corporate and municipal debt.

In other words, there is no guarantee that the interest rates individuals pay for home mortgages, auto loans, student debt, or credit cards would fall substantially or immediately under the FairTax. Further, nothing would force lenders holding existing loans (money already borrowed) to lower the rates consumers have already agreed to.

While FairTax advocates argue that competitive market forces would quickly drive these rates down, this also assumes that investors would be able to refinance or move their debt to another company. But, if the recent prolonged credit crisis has taught us anything, it's that the ability to alter one's existing loan agreements is far from being a sure thing.

The Least You Need to Know

- Under the FairTax, your expenses would likely stay the same or slightly increase, while your take-home pay would increase to sufficiently cover these amounts.

- The mortgage interest deduction, though lost under the FairTax, is not nearly as valuable as most Americans imagine, and the increase in take-home pay would likely make up for it.

- The prebate covers the FairTax charged on every household's expenses up to the federal poverty guidelines.

- With a transition to the FairTax, most likely the investment markets would remain relatively stable.

- The housing market, due primarily to the illiquidity of homes, might experience a shunning of newer homes subject to the FairTax.

- Interest rates are not likely to drop nearly as much as FairTax advocates predict, especially for consumers already locked into their loan or credit card terms.

Four Families Under the FairTax

In This Chapter

- A single mom gets a raise
- More dollars for blue collars
- The Riches—fairest in the land
- Retirees and the FairTax

One of the challenges of evaluating the effects of dueling tax policies is that much of the discussion revolves around theories and complex rules. Even the more concrete details, such as the prebate, can seem elusive until one sees them on paper.

To help you get a better handle on what the FairTax might mean for you, let's take a look at four different families under both systems. Here are the basic facts about each family:

- **The Tuff family**—A single mom raising two kids on an income of $30,000 per year. Ms. Tuff has no deductions and claims the Earned Income Credit (EIC).

- **The Middle family**—A blue-collar family raising two kids on an income of $60,000 per year. The Middle family takes $20,000 in deductions, including their home mortgage and donations to their church.

- **The Rich family**—The parents of two children and owners of a successful shoe store that provides net profits of $150,000 per year on sales of $300,000. They also receive $10,000 in investment income from their portfolio and claim $50,000 in deductions, including their mortgage.

- **The Greys**—A retired couple living on $3,000 per month in Social Security and their $250,000 nest egg in tax-deferred retirement accounts. They have occasional medical expenses but not enough to itemize their deductions.

The Tuff Family

Upon hearing about the FairTax, Ms. Tuff felt like she wanted to scream. The idea of adding an additional 23 percent inclusive sales tax (which raises the actual price of a good by 30 percent) to her expenses sounds beyond unmanageable. Further, since she gets money back each year when she files her taxes, the idea of this coming to an end sounds like things will only get tighter.

Of course, Ms. Tuff is a little intrigued at the idea of a monthly prebate and likes the idea of not paying Social Security taxes anymore. But she's not convinced that the prebate and the lack of taxes being withheld from her paycheck will cover the addition of the 23 percent FairTax to her expenses.

Your Wallet

Adopting the FairTax will not eliminate any of the Social Services programs many lower-income families have come to rely on, such as Food Stamps; the Special Supplemental Nutrition Program for Women, Infants, and Children (WIC); and unemployment compensation.

The Tuff Family Under the Current System

Under the current system, Ms. Tuff has no federal income taxes withheld from her paycheck since her income is low enough that she'll more than likely pay no income taxes. However, 7.65 percent of her paycheck is withheld for Social Security and Medicare, leaving her with $27,705 in take-home pay for the year or $2,308.75 per month.

At the end of 2008 when she files her taxes, Ms. Tuff reports taxable income of $11,500. This is calculated by subtracting the $8,000 standard deduction for her head of household status and three $3,500 personal exemptions (one for her and each of her children).

This level of taxable income translates into $1,156 in federal income tax for Ms. Tuff. However, she is eligible for the Child Tax Credit in the amount of $1,000 for each of her two children, as well as an

Earned Income Credit of $1,816. These combine to result in Ms. Tuff actually getting a refund of $2,660 instead of owing $1,156.

Considering that Ms. Tuff paid $2,295 in Social Security and Medicare taxes and received $2,660 in refunds under the current system, the U.S. tax system actually put a little bit of money ($365 for the year, or $30.41 per month) into her pocket. So it's understandable that she's a little apprehensive about ditching the current tax system.

To Be Fair

The examples used in this book do not include the Federal Child and Dependent Care Credit, which helps working parents recover some of the cost of daycare. Had this credit been included in the examples, the FairTax would look slightly less attractive versus the current system.

The Tuff Family Under the FairTax

Since the FairTax plan does not tax any wages, Ms. Tuff's take-home pay for the year (excluding state income taxes) is the same as her promised salary of $2,500 per month ($30,000 per year).

In addition to keeping her entire paycheck, Ms. Tuff would receive a prebate under the FairTax. According to the prebate formula from Chapter 4, she would receive $4,048 per year, or $337.33 per month.

Combined with keeping her entire paycheck each month, Ms. Tuff would have disposable income of $2,837.33 per month thanks to the prebate, versus $2,530.41 under the current tax system. This definitely makes the FairTax look like a better system for her than the existing U.S. tax code.

But it is important to incorporate the potential increases to price that could occur under the FairTax. While it's likely that prices will drop some due to the removal of embedded taxes, that's not guaranteed. Further, remember that a business has to raise its prices by 30 percent from its desired revenue level to ensure that the removal of a 23 percent tax doesn't hurt its profits. With this in mind, it would be useful to know how much prices could potentially increase (assuming she bought all new goods) without erasing all the benefit of the FairTax.

In Ms. Tuff's case, the difference between her monthly disposable income under the FairTax and the current system is $306.92. That means that prices could rise by this amount, or 12 percent, and still buy her the same amount of goods or services. In other words, if the enactment of the FairTax causes prices to rise by more than 12 percent, the benefits of the FairTax are erased and Ms. Tuff would've been better off under the existing system. If they rise by 12 percent or less or stay the same, she comes out ahead.

Your Wallet

Some critics of the FairTax claim that prices will drop only 10 percent due to the removal of embedded taxes, compared to the 22 percent estimated by many FairTax supporters. If these numbers hold true, the hard dollar value of the FairTax over the current system would be erased for families like the Tuffs.

The Middle Family

The Middle family were early advocates of the FairTax. They believe too much of their paycheck disappears to taxes and that other people don't pull their economic weight because they make too little or use tax loopholes to shield their large incomes. Under the FairTax, they think prices will go down, productivity will go up, and their lives will change dramatically for the better.

The Middle Family Under the Current System

Both Mr. and Mrs. Middle work 9-to-5 jobs in small-town America, and each get paid $30,000 per year. In addition to roughly $250 federal income tax withholding ($500 combined) that is removed from their paychecks, they also each have $191.25 removed for Social Security and Medicare ($382.50 for both). Thus, their monthly take-home pay is $4,117.50.

At 2008 tax time, the Middles report taxable income of $26,000 ($60,000 in income minus $20,000 in various deductions and four personal exemptions of $3,500 each). This leaves them owing $1,101 in income taxes after they take their permitted Child Tax Credit. Since the Middles make more than the EIC limit, they do not receive the refundable EIC as Ms. Tuff did. Of course, since they overpaid into the tax system through their payroll withholding ($6,600 for the year), they're entitled to a refund of their money in the amount of $5,499.

So when the smoke clears, the Middles paid $5,691 in combined income taxes ($1,101) and FICA payroll taxes ($4,590). That means their true take-home pay is not $60,000 but $54,309, which translates into a monthly disposable income of $4,525.75.

To Be Fair

While it seems highly unlikely, some fans of the FairTax argue that employers will raise employees' pay thanks to no longer having to contribute to FICA. For the employers of Mr. and Mrs. Middle, this represents roughly $4,500 in savings that could be funneled back into employee compensation.

The Middle Family Under the FairTax

Under the FairTax, the Middle family keeps their entire paycheck of $5,000 per month or $60,000 per year. To this, they get to add a prebate of $536.66, for a total monthly disposable income of $5,536. Therefore, the Middles would have roughly $1,010 more in disposable monthly income than under the current system.

Again, it is important to account for the fact that the removal of embedded taxes in the cost of goods and services may not drop nearly enough to absorb the 30 percent increase required to accommodate the 23 percent inclusive sales tax. If this is the case, there would be a unique break-even point for the Middle family, where they would have been better under the previous system. In this case, if they purchase only new goods and the average cost of the goods rises by more than 22 percent, they would've been better off under the previous system.

The Rich Family

Since the Rich family owns a retail business and hears customers complain daily about the amount of sales tax added to their purchases, they were extremely leery of a 23 percent national sales tax. Yet, at the same time, the idea of not having to pay double the FICA taxes that most people pay due to their self-employed status has left the Riches open to learning more about the FairTax.

The Rich Family Under the Current System

Clearly, the Rich family falls into the category of taxpayers who carry the largest percentage of

America's tax burden. First, since Mrs. Rich receives a salary of $150,000 from their business, she pays $12,648 in Social Security tax (using the maximum 2008 wage base of $102,000) and $3,600 in Medicare taxes (not subject to limits), for a grand total of $16,665.

Your Wallet

One strategy employed by married business owners such as the Riches is to have one employee receive the entire paycheck in order to push as much compensation as possible over the Social Security wage limit. By having Mrs. Rich receive the entire paycheck, the family pays Social Security only on $102,000. If they each received a $75,000 paycheck, they'd pay Social Security taxes on the entire amount ($150,000).

In addition to this, the Rich family reports a taxable income of $87,667 (their $150,000 in business income and $10,000 in investment income, less $50,000, four personal exemptions of $3,500 each, and an adjustment for half their self-employment taxes). This leaves them owing $14,606 in federal income taxes on top of their $16,665 in Social Security/Medicare taxes, for a grand total of $31,271. Yikes!

After that substantial haircut due to taxes, their effective take-home pay is $128,279 per year, or

$10,727.41 per month. That's a decrease in take-home pay of $2,605.92 per month versus their actual earnings.

The Rich Family Under the FairTax

The critique that the wealthiest in our country benefit the most under the FairTax finds firm footing when we look at how much it saves the Rich family. Of course, that doesn't mean the FairTax is faulted—perhaps just the opposite. FairTax proponents (along with the Rich family, most likely) would argue that the Riches are only saving so much because they're being freed from the huge burden that is unfairly placed on them.

Under the FairTax, the Rich family would keep the entire $160,000 in net income that comes into their household. Further, just like the Middle family of the same size, the Riches would receive a monthly prebate of $536.66, for a grand total of $166,439.92 in disposable income for the year, compared to $128,279 under the existing tax code. That translates into $13,869.99 per month, versus $10,727.41 under the current system—an increase of $3,142.58 per month.

So the question arises again of how this family would fare if prices on goods and services do not drop as expected. For the Rich family, prices would have to rise more than 29 percent for them to come out with less purchasing power under the FairTax than under the current system. Considering that the FairTax itself will raise the price of goods a maximum of 30 percent, this means that the wealthy, especially business owners, are the most insulated from the economic estimates used with the FairTax being incorrect.

Sweetening this deal is the fact that the Riches get to keep one quarter of 1 percent of their sales (subtracted from the 23 percent FairTax they must submit) as their compensation for collecting the FairTax. Since their business collects $300,000 in gross revenue, this would yield an administration fee of $750 that goes to the Riches. While that's not quite the same as winning the lottery, it's still money in their pockets.

The Greys

The Greys are petrified when they consider the FairTax. Unlike our other families, they're well past their working years and living off a fixed income comprised of their Social Security and a $12,500 annual withdrawal from their $250,000 in tax-deferred IRAs. They currently pay very little in taxes despite having virtually no deductions and are fearful that the FairTax will put them in the poorhouse or out on the street.

The Greys Under the Current System

With their annual income of $48,500 ($36,000 in Social Security plus $12,500 in taxable IRA withdrawals) and no deductions, it would seem that the Greys would owe some taxes. But the Greys, like many retirees, are not taxed on their Social Security benefits because they are below certain limits for their total income. Thus, what little income that is taxable (the IRA withdrawal) is zeroed out by their standard deductions and exemptions. In other words, under the current system, they owe nothing.

> **To Be Fair**
>
> The Greys did not receive an EIC because they're over the eligibility age of 65. However, since early retirees may still be eligible for the EIC, the benefit gained on the FairTax over the current system could potentially be much less for those still under 65.

The Greys Under the FairTax

Since there is no taxation on Social Security income or IRA withdrawals under the FairTax, the entire income of Mr. and Mrs. Grey remains untaxed. In addition, they would receive a monthly prebate of $398.66, or roughly $4,784 per year.

The only way the Greys would do worse under the FairTax is if the costs of goods and services did not drop sufficiently to absorb the cost of the FairTax. In other words, an increase in prices greater than approximately 10 percent would result in a loss of their spending power. This essentially puts them at greater risk of a loss of purchasing power than Ms. Tuff, who could tolerate a 12 percent rise in prices.

Comparing the Four Families

First, it is important to recognize these examples for what they are: a simplistic snapshot of four extremely unique financial situations. In addition to being slightly different from the finances of each unique reader of this book, these examples assumed that the families purchased all new goods and services, forcing their entire disposable income to be subject to the FairTax. In reality, some used goods would be mixed in with their purchases, which would raise the level of the price increase they could tolerate. Having said that, two things seem to be clear about the FairTax.

First, the FairTax accomplishes much of its goal of creating fairness in the tax system. The higher-income earners, who previously shouldered a much higher percentage of the nation's tax revenue, have recaptured a good deal of their disposable income. While the FairTax is not truly a flat tax (more on this in Chapter 10), it will still bring joy to the hearts of many overburdened high-income earners.

Second, if the FairTax advocates are wrong in their assertion that embedded taxes will cause the prices of goods to decrease by 22 percent, the FairTax may actually erode everyone's spending power, especially for lower-income earners and seniors. Again, this is not necessarily a reason to vote against the FairTax, but an invitation to truly investigate these risks more.

The Least You Need to Know

- To compare the FairTax versus the current system, calculate your house's monthly disposable income under each system.

- Though the FairTax comes out ahead in most examples, that also assumes a perfect scenario of no price increases, which would erase some or all of the benefit.

- Low-income families would most likely experience an increase to their disposable income under the FairTax.

- High-income earners and successful business owners would seem to gain the most from the FairTax replacing our arguably unfair progressive tax rate system.

- Retirees living primarily off of nontaxable Social Security income may be the most sensitive to any increase in the price of goods and services.

The Economic Effects of the FairTax

In This Chapter

- How much will the FairTax bring in?
- The economic fireworks of the FairTax
- FairTax promises too big to keep
- Funding key programs under the FairTax
- Death of the tax preparation industry
- The FairTax and charitable giving

In the 1990 Arnold Schwarzenegger classic movie *Total Recall*, a battle raged on the planet Mars over a giant reactor built by aliens millions of years before man's arrival. One faction believed that turning on the reactor would destroy the entire planet, while the other faction was convinced that it would save it. Minus the aliens, the FairTax situation isn't much different.

For those who believe in the FairTax, "turning it on" would most assuredly save our economy through unprecedented growth, record foreign investment, and the return of jobs that have been shipped overseas. For those who fear the FairTax, turning it on would result in a financial meltdown of unparalleled magnitude—an end to capitalism as we know it.

So, which is it? Like prices, wages, and the investment markets, the answer is probably somewhere near the middle. In other words, the FairTax would likely carry with it some economic benefits, but not the monumental economic windfall predicted by many. Further, some of the economic fireworks promised under the FairTax are likely to fizzle under the constraints of reality. Likewise, the financial apocalypse that many are sure the FairTax will usher in is simply rubbish, especially compared to the train wreck our current system already is.

FairTax Revenue Estimates

The biggest single premise underlying the promises FairTax advocates provide is that the FairTax is *revenue neutral*. In other words, it would not collect more or less revenue than it now collects under the current system, but simply collect it in a different (and more fair) manner. Whether or not this statement is true is one of the primary jumping off points for evaluating how the FairTax affects the rest of the economy. If it's not close to revenue neutral, it goes from being a nice idea to something that could put our economy in harm's way.

According to the Congressional Budget Office (CBO), the estimated total collections for 2010 for all income, estate, gift, and Social Security taxes will be roughly $2.6 trillion and account for almost

95 percent of the U.S. government's revenue. This amounts to roughly 17.2 percent of the U.S. gross domestic product, which is the total cost of all goods and services sold in the United States during the year. If the FairTax is revenue neutral as many propose, it would have to bring in roughly this same amount.

def•i•ni•tion

> **Revenue neutral** means that a proposed alternative tax system does not collect more or less than it does under the current system. It may collect the money in a different manner, but the overall amount collected is the same.

According to a study done by Suffolk University economist Paul Bachman and his associates, the adjusted tax base on which the FairTax would be charged (which includes things like government spending and removes things like the prebate and the cost of the IRS) is equivalent to somewhere between $9 and $10 trillion under our current system. That is to say that all spending subject to the FairTax is roughly $9 to $10 trillion annually in the United States.

Of course, that number currently has embedded taxes included in it, which many believe would be removed at the same time the FairTax is added. Under estimates used by FairTax-sponsored economists, the removal of these embedded taxes would amount to an estimated 22 percent drop in prices or an adjusted total FairTax base of $7 to $7.8 trillion.

To collect an inclusive tax of 23 percent on this $7 to $7.8 trillion, the prices of all goods and services sold would be increased by roughly 30 percent to $9.1 to $10.1 trillion, or back where they started. Applying the 23 percent FairTax to this would in turn yield revenue for the government in the ballpark of $2.1 to $2.3 trillion.

Thus, comparing them side-by-side, we find that the current U.S. tax system brings in about $2.6 trillion per year, and the FairTax is estimated to bring in about $2.1 to $2.3 trillion. While these numbers are not identical, they're still close enough that many people (myself included) believe that the FairTax generally lives up to its promise of being revenue neutral.

To Be Fair

Many critics have argued that what is taken in under the FairTax would drop dramatically in a severe recession as people spend less, leading to a revenue shortfall for the government. The reality, however, is that income tax collections would fall in a similar fashion since people make less money, corporations report lower profits, and investments lose money instead of gain. In the end, an economic downturn would substantially affect both systems.

FairTax Fireworks or Fizzle?

If you visited one of the tax tea parties in early 2009, you heard a lot of talk about how this revenue neutral FairTax will save the economy and secure America's head seat at the global financial table. You might have been told that, thanks to the increase in take-home pay, the removal of forced personal and corporate income taxes, and the influx of global business the FairTax would supposedly bring, the economy has nowhere to go but up. You were also told that worker productivity would naturally climb when you remove taxation from the fruit of their labors. Of course, FairTax critics call these statements wishful thinking, unrealistic, and ignorant of economics.

In reality, the likelihood of the FairTax pushing the economy through the roof, as well as it being a complete economic dud, is low. As mentioned before, the FairTax is much more likely to have a varied effect, with a small positive overall effect to the economy.

The problem with both sides is that their economic assumptions are simply that, economic assumptions. They assume simple causality (if "this" happens, then "that" will surely follow) and closed systems (the only variables that will have an effect are the ones our study considers). In reality, there are just too many variables to account for, and many economists' closed systems don't allow for the human nature of choices.

Firework #1: Increased Exports, Fewer Imports

The FairTax's most legitimate chance to contribute to economic growth comes from its ability to change the balance of U.S. foreign trade—injecting new money into our economy from other nations' consumers while also raising the competitiveness of our own goods against imports. The source for this increased competitiveness is the belief that U.S. goods will finally be able to compete on equal footing with foreign goods, something the current tax code impedes.

To Be Fair

While FairTax supporters are quick to point out that rebalancing the $750 billion trade deficit could dramatically change the U.S. economy, it's important to realize that a large, overnight change is unlikely. This is due to the fact that more than 50 percent of the trade deficit comes from imported oil, with another 10 percent coming from imported cars. Since the import of these two things is not likely to drop overnight, a dramatic rebalancing is less likely than a gradual one.

First, FairTax supporters point out that goods exported to other countries do not get taxed under the FairTax. This essentially discounts them by the level of embedded taxes removed, roughly 22 percent, without affecting the profit margins of U.S. companies. If this holds true, it's hard to believe that there won't be a boost in demand for some U.S. products.

Of course, the key phrase, the one that would likely keep the economic gains from being off the charts, is that demand would increase for only some U.S. products. In other words, the only real economic gain would come from foreign consumers buying more of our products than they already do now. If the rest of the world still views U.S.-manufactured cars as second-rate, for example, a 22 percent discount is not likely to change the level of demand dramatically from what it is now.

Second, with regard to U.S. consumers, the prices of goods manufactured in the United States would now stand toe-to-toe with those manufactured in countries that exempt exported goods from things like a value-added tax (VAT). These foreign goods have had little or no embedded taxes in their prices when they show up on our shores, compared to our own goods that currently do. By removing the embedded taxes from our goods as well, imported goods will lose any tax-based price advantage they had, increasing the demand for some domestic alternatives. In turn, this would keep more money in our economy, which can result in a stronger economic bottom line.

Firework #2: Relocation of Foreign Businesses

The last couple of decades have seen numerous foreign manufacturers relocating factories to the United States to save significant money on operations that serve our market anyway. For example, major foreign auto manufacturers have relocated manufacturing plants to the United States, which saves them the trouble of shipping their finished product halfway around the world.

The FairTax would most definitely spur such relocations, since goods produced here would now be free from embedded taxes. This would let some foreign companies effectively produce their goods that they sell here and elsewhere at a cheaper rate than in their home countries. Further, the money earned by nonresident employees of relocating companies would get taxed under the FairTax as it is spent, raising the level of revenue.

Firework #3: Offshore Money Moves Home

Another opportunity to introduce new money into our economic system, something that could truly spur economic growth, is the repatriation of offshore money. This is money that's been moved to banks outside the United States either legally (corporations conducting business outside the United States) or illegally (individuals seeking to avoid taxation and protect themselves from lawsuits).

Estimates typically put the value of U.S. money held offshore at roughly $1 trillion, which represents about $\frac{1}{30}$ of the total value of the U.S. stock markets and all bank deposits combined. The IRS has estimated that this represents a loss of roughly $70 billion annually in collections revenue.

Thus, if even a portion of this money moves back into the economy, it could lead to a short-term strengthening in our country's investment and banking activities. But getting people to move their money back to the United States is easier said than done and would likely happen over time instead of overnight.

In the case of assets legally held by corporations through their foreign subsidiaries, the FairTax would likely encourage an influx of some or all of this cash into the U.S. economy. The catalyst for this is that these assets will no longer be taxed any differently on their income, whether they're held in the United States or by an offshore subsidiary, because they won't, in fact, be taxed at all. Likewise, when they are spent in the United States, they'll be taxed the same under the FairTax, regardless of where they were held. In short, holding money offshore would become more complex and costly than simply holding it in the United States.

To Be Fair

Even though U.S. citizens hold assets offshore, these assets still affect our economy. Many of these offshore accounts still invest in American markets through offshore mutual funds made available by U.S. mutual fund companies. Further, many of these offshore banks provide credit cards that allow citizens to spend their hidden money on expenses incurred on U.S. soil.

In the case of individual assets illegally moved offshore, they won't all quickly return home unless some kind of amnesty or forgiveness is outlined for these account holders. Though it may be more attractive or convenient to move these assets back to the United States from a financial perspective, the fact is that they broke U.S. tax and banking laws, something the government has been active in prosecuting in recent years. To move a large amount of money back onshore is to remove the cloak of invisibility that has protected these tax cheats from prosecution.

That's not to say that the FairTax wouldn't eventually put an end to illegal offshore banking and keep more money directly working in our economy. Rather, it does say that people would no longer have an incentive to move new funds offshore and would likely trickle money back into the economy over time.

Fizzle #1: The Removal of Personal Tax Barriers

One of the highly praised features of the FairTax, one that its supporters believe will knock the economy into overdrive, is the removal of tax barriers to certain activities. Likewise, those who are worried that the FairTax will harm the economy are quick to criticize certain tax barriers that are created, such as the taxation of service industries.

While both sides have valid points—that barriers to certain activities (or the removal of them) can in fact influence people's financial choices—it's important to realize that these only matter to a degree. In reality, the addition of some barriers wouldn't keep people from engaging in certain necessary activities, and the removal of barriers would not necessarily result in people pursuing certain activities beyond reason or need.

To Be Fair

The FairTax also may add a potential psychological barrier to economic growth, in that consumers who have long viewed sales taxes as a negative thing would actually spend less on new goods, shop harder for used goods, and even shop overseas or across borders to avoid the FairTax. If this is the case, the amount of revenue collected could drop noticeably.

For example, some argue that the elimination of income tax under the FairTax, including those on investment gains, would encourage people to both work harder and invest more. While this seems to make sense on paper, the reality is that there are forces that will naturally limit these activities, even if all the tax barriers to these activities are removed.

In reality, the amount that people work is primarily limited by the principle of diminishing marginal returns. This principle states what many of us already know—that after working a certain number of hours (or eating a certain number of donuts or opening a certain number of birthday presents), the excitement wears off. In turn, the "reward" we feel for working additional hours and making additional money begins to decrease. This is especially true when other valuable activities compete for our time. Thus, the absence of income taxes won't inspire people who have been working exhausting 40-hour weeks to suddenly begin working 60-hour weeks.

The FairTax's effect on the nation's investing habits is not likely to be much different. Those who can invest and save are already doing so in a manner consistent with their own internal sense of motivation and reward, not the tax code. Those that don't or can't invest aren't likely to suddenly change their personal financial habits just because the tax code has changed.

I've witnessed this in my own professional experience with the introduction of Roth IRAs in 1997. Though these accounts offered juicy tax benefits over the existing Traditional IRAs, the typical non-saver didn't stop spending (or wasting) money on other things and start investing. The only thing that really changed is that existing savers began using these accounts instead of the older Traditional IRAs. In the end, roughly the same amount of money was being invested by the same people as before the favorable tax law change, just in a slightly different manner.

Your Wallet

The amount of money people are taxed (under the FairTax or our current system) doesn't change the fact that many people who would like to work more hours and make more money can't, because the work is simply not available. In essence, providing a greater incentive to work (as the FairTax claims to do) makes no difference if no additional work can be found.

Fizzle #2: Growth Requires New Money

One of the key ingredients necessary for true economic growth is an influx of new money, something the FairTax causes in only isolated circumstances: more favorable export environment, foreign companies relocating, etc. In other words, if all people do is trade the same money back and forth, with the government taking a portion each time for the FairTax, it's hard for true growth to occur. It doesn't matter if the tax system encourages people to hand the money back and forth more often or not.

Now granted, people may bid up the prices on goods or investment assets as they buy from each other, creating a false sense of new wealth. *But that doesn't equal growth.* If anything, it equals the creation of an unsustainable economic bubble. For true growth to occur, new money not previously part of the economy has to be introduced into it. And since this can only come from the U.S. Treasury printing money (which can cause inflation), the conversion of raw materials into goods of value (something most modern workers no longer can influence for their own gain), the loosening of economic policy, or non-U.S. money flooding our economy, a runaway boom under the FairTax doesn't seem feasible.

To illustrate this point, let's look at a very simplistic example. Let's say you sell hats and I sell umbrellas, both for $10 each, with the 23 percent FairTax included in that price. Let's also say that we each have $100 in the bank (or $200 total between us) that we've earned from selling our goods.

Now let's say you buy an umbrella from me, and I buy a hat from you—we each pay $10 out of our bank account, receive $10 from the other person, and also send $2.30 in FairTax to the government. After one transaction, we each have spent $10, but only earned $7.70 when the taxes due are figured in. That means each of our bank accounts just shrank by $2.30 to $97.70.

Now, let's say, in addition to us buying and selling hats and umbrellas every day, the government sends the taxes we've been collecting to a senior citizen as Social Security. Then that senior citizen comes in and blows all his money on our hats and umbrellas. In a best-case scenario, we've done nothing but simply recover the money we started with. No new wealth has been created, despite what seems to have been a busy period for our little imaginary economy.

Again, this is an example of why the FairTax (as well as our current income tax system) has no real ability to create wealth across the whole economy over time by simply altering the rates or method of collection. That's not to say that savvy business owners and investors can't accumulate more of the wealth than others, but in the overall modern economy, the same finite amount of wealth generally exists.

Thus, the only way for the FairTax to truly cause economic growth is to create an environment where money from outside our economy finds its way in. Although this is likely to increase some under the FairTax, it's unlikely that most of the world's capital is going to flow into the United States in an unprecedented or continuous way.

Fizzle #3: Lost Jobs Return to the United States

Another promise FairTax supporters make that is likely more fizzle than fireworks is the return of jobs lost to other countries. That's not because the FairTax, especially in its attraction of foreign business, won't create some jobs but rather because many U.S. jobs are most likely forever lost to our economy due to the extremely low wages found internationally.

Not taxing individual income would make no real difference in the fact that a customer service representative in India costs $2 per hour, while one in Indiana costs $10 per hour (plus employee benefits). If there is a 22 percent drop in the price of U.S. goods and services as some FairTax advocates predict, our basic labor will still cost three to four times as much.

Additionally, any new jobs created within the United States by foreign companies relocating will face two hurdles in their ability to push the economy above and beyond where it is now. First, many of these jobs will likely be absorbed by the 500,000 to 1,000,000 U.S. workers displaced by the death of the tax preparation industry. Second, many of these foreign corporations will reserve the juiciest jobs for their current employees who are willing to relocate to America.

Big-Ticket Economic Issues

Because many people have expressed concern or hope about some big-ticket economic issues under the proposed FairTax, no discussion of the FairTax would be complete without touching on its effects on the funding of the Social Security system, the reduction of the national debt, and donations to nonprofit organizations.

Social Security and Medicare Funding

While many people try to make a mountain out of this molehill, the FairTax would not likely make any difference in the overall funding of Social Security or Medicare. That's because the FairTax's rate formula would be reset annually to collect the same amount of revenue that would have been collected under our existing system. In other words, the FairTax will not likely surprise us by collecting hundreds of billions of dollars extra for Social Security in a good year.

The case some FairTax advocates make is that the booming economy created by the FairTax will pump more revenue into the Social Security system, although this seems to run against their revenue neutral premise.

The case made against the FairTax and Social Security funding is that it would likely go underfunded if not enough revenue is collected. But again, with the actual rate being reset each year to match what should have been collected under our current system, a monumental shortfall is highly unlikely. In the end, a hope or fear of how the FairTax will affect Social Security is probably unfounded.

Your Wallet

The Medicare contribution, whether made through payroll deductions under our current system or through the FairTax, primarily pays for Hospitalization Insurance (Medicare Part A). Routine medical care for seniors is actually funded by Medicare Part B, which actually requires all participating seniors to pay a monthly premium— something that can and will likely go up, regardless of which tax system we use.

The Reduction of the National Debt

If there's one thing that truly scares many economists more than bad tax policy or the Social Security shortfall, it's the national debt. The United States continues to fund much of its existence by borrowing money from its future (by selling Treasury bonds) to fund its existence today, with both political parties carrying their fair share of responsibility.

While some are rightfully alarmed that the national debt is teetering on being equal to 100 percent of the annual gross domestic product of the United States, the bigger problem is the actual cost to service this debt. In 2008, the interest paid on this debt was roughly $400 billion or 16 percent of the total revenue the U.S. government brought in. If something is not done to curb the growth of the national debt and begin paying down what we owe, the annual cost of this debt will leave little money for anything else.

Supporters and critics of the FairTax once again seem to take the side of extreme pessimism or optimism. FairTax advocates claim (again in spite of their pitch of revenue neutrality) the FairTax would lead to increased revenue over time, which would lower the need for borrowing and even aid to the repayment of this debt.

Of course, critics argue that the revenue collected will not be sufficient, only adding to the country's need to borrow and growing inability to serve both its debt and its citizens.

In reality, the elimination of the national debt will likely have very little to do with the current tax system or the proposed alternatives. Rather, it will have to do with politicians (at the prompting of the rest of us) reeling in their spending over time. Chances are that if any tax system, either by design or by accident, increases our nation's tax revenue, it'll get spent unless politicians commit to do otherwise.

Charitable Giving to Nonprofits

One major economic complaint about the FairTax, which seems to show a lack of understanding about charity by many, is that the loss of the deduction for charitable giving under the FairTax proposal will leave charities high and dry. This in turn would have a broad economic impact because charities in general take an immense amount of pressure off the government's budget when it comes to social programs, funding education, etc. Moreover, some have even criticized the FairTax as antireligion since they fear the elimination of the charitable deduction will put pressure on church budgets.

Having personally worked in and managed non-profits for nearly a decade of my life, I, and so many others, can tell you this is just not the case. In reality, most people give because they feel called to give, whether by their sense of community, their desire to give back, or out of religious obligation. The deduction, while an added bonus, is just that, a bonus.

To Be Fair

The FairTax repeals the IRS regulation against churches advocating a specific political viewpoint or endorsing candidates. While some welcome this freedom, others are concerned that the FairTax dangerously closes the gap between church and state.

Ironically, since many Americans who donate money to their causes of choice don't have enough other deductions to itemize on their tax return, they end up taking the standard deduction anyway. In other words, their charitable contributions end up saving them nothing on their tax returns, making the deduction irrelevant.

In all likelihood, charitable deductions will continue under the FairTax at roughly the same pace they have now. The only minor difference might be what is donated, such as cash versus appreciated property. Under the current system, it's more favorable to donate $1,000 in appreciated stock than it is $1,000 in cash, since a taxpayer would avoid paying capital gains tax on the donated stock. Under the FairTax, where investment gains are not taxed, it would be just as efficient for some people to donate cash as it would be stock, real estate, or other valuable property.

The Death of the IRS and Tax Industries

While most Americans would not shed a tear over the elimination of the IRS under the FairTax, when one puts a human face to the job loss, it can definitely take one's breath away. In addition to the 110,000 to 115,000 jobs lost at the IRS, it is estimated that there are roughly 170,000 CPAs and 40,000 *Enrolled Agents* whose primary revenue source is tax preparation. Add to this the number of support staff that serve these professionals, the vast number of state-licensed tax preparers, and the companies who design software and publish tax-related materials, and the job loss could easily exceed one million jobs.

def•i•ni•tion

Enrolled Agents do not directly work for the IRS, but rather are a class of tax professionals licensed by the IRS to prepare taxes and represent taxpayers before the IRS. In fact, they are the only group of for-profit tax practitioners that are administered an exam by the IRS testing their knowledge in the area of taxation.

While some of these professionals have skills that would easily cross over into other fields, some would have their life's work and careers flushed down the drain. For these individuals, the enactment of the FairTax would be a dark day and would result in financial upheaval for their families. While none would likely end up homeless, it's likely that many would take a permanent pay cut. These pay cuts would not hurt the overall economy, however, as it would also represent billions of dollars that consumers could spend on something else besides tax preparation.

Does this mean we shouldn't enact the FairTax in order to save these jobs? Not at all. If the FairTax is the right direction for the country and ultimately creates a more fair and equitable tax system, then we should embrace it. Not doing so would be the equivalent of allowing the asbestos industry to continue unchecked in order to save the jobs of its workers. In the end, we must place the overall health of the economy first.

The Least You Need to Know

- The FairTax comes close to living up to its promise of being revenue neutral.

- A more favorable environment for U.S. exports, foreign companies doing business in the United States, and offshore money could give our economy a reasonable boost.

- The hope of recovering jobs previously lost overseas and of workers lining up to work longer and harder is unlikely to pan out.

- The FairTax or any other system will not resolve the Social Security and national debt problems; only politicians changing their mindsets can do that.

- Charitable giving will likely remain steady, even under the FairTax.

Chapter 7

The Political Effects of the FairTax

In This Chapter

- Say goodbye to vote buying
- The possibility for greater transparency
- Things the FairTax doesn't address
- The case for increased voter involvement

When you stop to consider the potential political effects of the FairTax, you've got to wonder if the politicians supporting it really know what they're getting themselves into! All joking aside, it wouldn't come as a surprise to discover that many politicians' resistance to the FairTax is rooted in their fear of what it means for the power they hold. That's not to say that many politicians aren't voicing otherwise legitimate arguments, but it's to say they're also very thankful for some legitimate arguments to hide behind.

To a large degree, today's politicians remind me of those in ancient Rome who threw bread to starving crowds, who thought of themselves as saviors simply because they handed them the crumbs after mismanaging the loaves. Today, instead of throwing us bread, they throw us tax breaks. Whether it's a tax break here, a stimulus check there, or even a refund of our own money we loaned them interest-free all year, we tend to thank the government for these "freebies." In reality, though, many of our politicians have been part of the gross mismanagement of a system that is too complex for the average citizen to hold them accountable for. Wherever you stand on the FairTax versus alternative systems, one of its great promises worth evaluating is how it refocuses much of the political process away from the discussion of tax policy and toward real change.

The FairTax and Vote Buying

Perhaps the biggest and most direct political promise of the FairTax is that it will largely end the process of "vote buying" by politicians. Under this very common political tactic, politicians grab chunks of the electorate by promising a change (or protection) of the tax code that benefits one group over another.

Before you think I'm harping on one political party over another or suggesting that some of their promised changes wouldn't be beneficial, just consider the recent history of vote buying:

- John McCain promised to keep President Bush's tax cuts intact, which primarily benefited the upper and middle classes.
- President Obama promised tax relief for 95 percent of Americans at the expense of the other 5 percent.

- President Clinton promised a "middle-class tax cut," which he failed to deliver.
- President Bush Sr. told us to read his lips and promised us "no new taxes." (He did, incidentally, raise taxes.)

In each case, these campaign tax promises translated directly into money placed into one class of voters' pockets. And while many people voted for these people for a variety of other reasons besides tax policy, it's undeniable that many were swayed solely on the promise of less taxes.

By overhauling and simplifying the tax system, whether with the FairTax or an alternative plan, much of the power to attract votes based on tax policies would be stripped away. That would undoubtedly leave the politicians having to battle over and make promises about problems more pressing in the national scheme of things.

That's not to say that some vote-buying opportunities wouldn't still exist under the FairTax, but they would be relatively small. For example, an opportunity arises from the combination of the fact that a portion of the FairTax collected is paid to the states and businesses that collect it and that government would be taxed on its expenditures just like individuals.

In other words, a politician who steers a billion-dollar fighter plane contract to a Southern California defense contractor would not only be guaranteeing both California and the company a juicy contract but also the ability to get paid for simply collecting the tax due on that contract. A billion-dollar contract would yield an additional $2.5 million in revenue for the state as well as for the company.

As mentioned, the amount of potential abuse here is relatively small since most government contracts are nowhere near that large. But in a desire for you to see this from all angles, it's definitely worth mentioning.

Increased Transparency—Maybe

One of the most deeply hoped-for by-products of the FairTax is increased transparency from our politicians. In large part, this would occur because tracking the amount of money collected under the FairTax is greatly simplified. Instead of having multiple tax codes, with multiple rates, with a large portion of the money changing hands around April 15th, it's simply 23 percent of qualifying goods and services collected at the point of sale throughout the year.

Unlike the current tax system, this would make collections under the FairTax very easy to report and track and very hard for politicians to get their hands on without some scrutiny. Thus, when a politician wants money for a project or program, he'd be asking for a sliver of the one pie through which all money flows in and out. Undoubtedly (thanks to the media) such a visible process would provide greater scrutiny over our current fragmented tax system.

Increased Scare Tactics

Because these politicians, attempting to grab a piece of the money pie, would receive greater scrutiny under the FairTax, those passionate about their pet projects would undoubtedly up the ante when it comes to scare tactics. In order to gain the public support to keep them in office as they spend, we might see these politicians paint even more dire pictures about what a failure to spend means.

Thus, one of the political drawbacks of the FairTax we must expect if it is passed is a constant ringing of the financial fire alarm. Expect to hear politicians engaged in heated debates about how "failure to spend on *this* right now will undoubtedly lead to *that* later." Expect to hear increased threats about the downfall of America, your safety, and the plight of different groups of people and programs. Expect it all because, ultimately, most politicians will never cease to be politicians.

Confusing Programs Will Remain Confusing

While the FairTax promises to greatly simplify the way America's tax revenue is calculated and collected, that means nothing in regard to simplifying the programs we spend it on. Social Security will continue to be a hotly contested mess, the Defense Department will likely continue to pay $600 for hammers, and the effectiveness of educational spending in our country will be as hard to measure as ever. The only thing the FairTax guarantees to do is to make it clear where the money for these programs is coming from.

In addition to not necessarily eliminating the confusion surrounding certain programs, we have no guarantees (only hopes) that the FairTax will affect any of the following:

- ***Pork*-filled legislation**—Nothing in the FairTax bill, despite many people's hopes, explicitly eliminates the ability of politicians to build slyly worded pork into their legislative agenda. Even under the FairTax, these programs will continue to exist as long as the American public lets politicians get away with them.

- ***Earmarks***—Like pork in general, there is nothing in the FairTax to keep politicians from engaging in the process of earmarking funds for pet projects in their home states or districts.

def•i•ni•tion

Pork, or pork barrel spending, refers to spending projects a politician includes in legislation meant to benefit a very small group of his constituents. Many times this pork comes in the form of **earmarks**, or portions of a spending bill that an elected official can direct toward pet projects without having to truly argue its merits. This is different from large-scale vote buying, when a politician is essentially trying to gain constituents by promising tax breaks or other benefits.

- **State financial problems**—In the last few
  years, state financial crises have grabbed
  as many headlines as the national financial
  situation. State after state is finding itself ill-
  prepared for economic slowdowns, forcing it
  to cut programs across the board. While the
  FairTax may increase state revenue somewhat due to its role in collecting the tax, it
  comes with no conditions on how the state
  needs to steward that money.

Increased Voter Involvement—Maybe

Another hope that FairTax fans hold out for is
greater voter involvement. In theory, when people
see their portion of the FairTax listed on their
receipts on a day-in, day-out basis, they'll be much
more adamant about how that money gets spent.
The hope is that they'll hold their politicians
accountable, quickly voting them out of office if
they spend frivolously or with bias.

Even more so, many of the FairTax proponents
hope that staring at their taxes face-to-face on a
daily basis as they spend will motivate the 40 percent of adult Americans who don't vote to get out
and do so. Of course, the irony is that that 40 percent may quickly decide they hate the FairTax, align
with those who were initially against it, and quickly
move to overturn it.

While there's no doubt that the potential for voter
involvement is increased with the FairTax, the

probability of it happening is still far less than 100 percent. That's because, unfortunately, many Americans are both apathetic about the political process and overwhelmed with life to the point that they cannot follow politics thoroughly. In the end, it's probably just as likely that under the FairTax the same political agendas would continue to duke it out, with no real increase in voter involvement.

The Least You Need to Know

- Politicians consistently use tax promises to buy votes, something that would likely be significantly reduced under the FairTax.

- The FairTax would increase the level of transparency about what money the government is collecting and, in turn, who is asking to use it.

- Political scare tactics have the potential to increase as politicians are forced to more visibly make the case for the portion of the revenue pie they wish to spend.

- Politicians will likely continue to bury pork and earmarks in more confusing bills and legislation, even under the FairTax.

- FairTax supporters believe that seeing the FairTax computed on the bottom of every receipt would prompt people to want greater involvement in how that money is spent.

8

Ethical Issues with the FairTax

In This Chapter

- Is a progressive tax system fair?
- A quick look at the Constitution
- Penalizing the risk-takers
- The survival of entitlement programs

Few political debates divide people into such clear-cut camps as taxes. Whether it's over who is taxed, who goes untaxed, or what the taxes are used for, angry citizens on both sides can find plenty of fodder. More than anything else, taxes have become a politicized version of that old beer commercial in which two groups of people stand around yelling "tastes great" and "less filling." Except in this instance, they're yelling "tax the rich" and "tax the poor." Indeed, the discussion of taxation for many now borders on which economic class should have their portion of the tax burden increased.

At the middle of this shouting match are both small business owners and entitlement programs, such as welfare, unemployment, Social Security, and other services (whose spiraling costs must be paid for by someone). Naturally, since the lower- and middle-class folks are barely scraping by, they're more than happy to shift the costs of these programs to business owners and the middle class and rich. Likewise, the middle class and rich, many of whom will never personally benefit from these programs, are much less excited to see their hard-earned money be used for these programs as opposed to things that reward them for taking enormous risks.

Despite what its name seems to imply, the FairTax is not necessarily an attempt to decrease the tax burden of these programs on the upper classes (though this would definitely be possible through careful planning). Rather, it is an attempt to tie the taxation necessary for these programs to what you spend rather than what you make, while substantially reducing the tax preparation burden and costs on American citizens and their businesses. This shift, which does not necessarily ease the burden on one group or raise it on another, is what the FairTax founders hope makes their system "fair."

Is Our Current Tax System Fair?

Under the current system of taxation, income is taxed in "brackets," or as I like to visualize them, "buckets." The money that falls into each bucket is taxed at that bucket's rate. Once that bucket is full, you begin filling up the next bucket, which is then taxed at a higher rate. Never is that higher rate applied backward or retroactively to the previous buckets that have already been filled up and taxed at a lower rate.

For example, under the 2009 tax code, the first $16,700 in taxable income is taxed at 10 percent for a married couple filing a joint return. All additional income, up to $69,700, is taxed at 15 percent, and so on. So if someone makes $50,000 in taxable income for the year, he pays 10 percent on the first $16,700 (or $1,670 in taxes) and 15 percent on the remaining $33,300 in income (or $4,995 in taxes), for a grand total of $6,665 in taxes on $50,000.

The idea that each subsequent bucket is taxed at a progressively higher rate is why our current system is *progressive*. But it's important to note that the FairTax still does tax people at progressively higher rates (in this case, on what they spend), thanks to the monthly FairTax prebate. But in this case, the FairTax system has only two buckets as opposed to the six buckets in the current system. So if you're hoping the FairTax will end "tax discrimination" against those who earn more money and want to enjoy the fruits of their labor, it won't. It essentially lets those who are at or below the poverty line avoid paying taxes, while taxing those above the poverty line on everything they spend. Thus, those who spend more will be taxed more.

def•i•ni•tion

Progressive tax systems theoretically tax each dollar earned over certain levels at a higher amount.

A Quick Look at the U.S. Constitution

Time and time again, I hear people argue about what the founding fathers would think of our relatively new progressive tax system (enacted in 1913), especially since we heavily use it to fund entitlement programs. Many would argue correctly that the United States was founded in part to escape tax tyranny, but incorrectly that the founding fathers were against all taxation and welfare programs.

So from a constitutional point of view, here are some things to keep in mind as you evaluate whether or not the FairTax is the most ethical system to replace our current system:

- **Welfare**—Both the Preamble of the Constitution and Article 1 explicitly give the government the right to tax the population to pay for the "national defense and common welfare." While many people wish to lump these together and say that taxation is meant to support only the military, most constitutional scholars and interstate highway drivers would happily disagree.

- **The Fourteenth Amendment**—This is perhaps one of the most overlooked pieces of the Constitution when it comes to taxation. This amendment, which is meant in part to protect individuals against discrimination, should also logically protect people who make more money from being taxed at a higher, discriminatory rate. While being taxed more because you make more isn't perhaps as vile a form of discrimination as racism, many would argue that it is discrimination nonetheless.

To Be Fair

Many historians would be quick to point out that the Boston Tea Party and the ensuing Revolutionary War were not so much about paying high taxes but rather because the colonists did not receive a voice or vote in the taxes that were collected. Thus, current voters who are unhappy with their tax situation are inaccurate in their assertion that they're being "taxed without representation," since they did, in fact, receive the chance to make their opinion known through voting.

- **The Sixteenth Amendment**—The original intent of the founding fathers was to have each state be liable for a portion of the national taxes, based on its population. In other words, states with a large population (and indirectly, the citizens living in those states) would be responsible for more of the federal income tax bill than people in places like South Dakota. The Sixteenth Amendment overturned this and allowed the government to levy taxes directly against an individual's income, without regard to what portion his state was liable for. As mentioned in Chapter 2, one of the goals of the FairTax is to immediately overturn the Sixteenth Amendment.

Welfare for the Rich

Many of those who rail against the current tax system as an unfair means of funding the lifestyles of people who are unwilling to work as hard fail to realize that many wealthier individuals also receive government subsidies that many lower-income Americans do not. While higher-income readers might be hard-pressed to think of the last "check" they received from Uncle Sam, the reality is that plenty of tax deductions and credits benefit only people with larger incomes.

For example, buying a home in America isn't as simple as having good enough credit to qualify for a loan. Many loans require anywhere from 3 to 20 percent of the home's value up front as a down payment. For higher-income wage earners who can trim some discretionary expenses and accumulate a down payment, their new mortgage permits them to deduct a portion of their monthly payments on their tax return. Taxpayers who cannot afford the down payment simply because of the inability to earn a higher wage or accumulate a down payment often end up paying a much higher after-tax cost for the same roof over their head.

This is just one example out of a hundred possible of how our current tax system gives opportunities to some people (both rich and poor) while leaving others (most often the middle class) footing the bill. Not only do many view this as unfair or unethical, they also recognize that it creates "vote-buying opportunities," which we talk about more in the next chapter.

Your Wallet

For those taxpayers who do not have enough deductible expenses to qualify for the same deductions as their wealthier counterparts, the government does provide a "standard deduction" that provides some tax relief. Further, above certain income levels, many of the deductions the wealthy receive begin to get "phased out" or reduced as their income climbs.

Taxing the Risk-Takers, Sometimes

One of the things that makes America unique is the ability to build a billion-dollar business out of your garage, with only hard work and wits as your initial investment. On their best days, capitalism and entrepreneurship drive everything from the economy to racial equality in our country. Thus, any stifling of this, be it through taxes or any other means, is arguably harmful for America.

Unfortunately, most business owners (from the smallest one-man companies to the largest shareholder-owned corporations) lose more money to taxes than just about any other expense. This is especially true for service-based businesses whose revenue is primarily built around the labor of the owner and his or her employees.

Some would make the ethical argument that it's unfair to levy the heaviest taxes on the people who bear the largest amount of financial risk in growing our economy. They'd declare that the reward for investing money in other people's businesses, much less starting their own business that potentially creates jobs, should not be the addition of taxes, but the removal of them. And while the current lower capital gains rate encourages this to some degree, things such as payroll taxes and corporate tax rates (for C corporations and personal service/ professional corporations) are downright frustrating for many.

Adding insult to injury is the fact that the government from time to time subsidizes certain industries through juicy tax breaks, but leaves others twisting in the wind. While there may be strategic reasons for encouraging certain industries, the use of selective taxation to aid those industries seems the height of unfairness to many struggling to keep the lights on. Retailers have recognized this for years as they've been forced to charge customers local and state income taxes, while many industries that provide services (doctors, lawyers, etc.) escape scot-free from sales tax.

While the FairTax does not eliminate America's tax burden by any stretch, it definitely has the potential to create a more ethical and tax-favorable environment for businesses. In essence, the tax burden on all businesses, regardless of their industry, is virtually removed.

While this might sound like a slam dunk, it's important to realize that the tax burden these businesses used to carry would be fully shifted to you as the consumer. And while FairTax proponents argue that prices should drop enough to make your overall cost the same, if they're wrong, it's coming out of your pocket.

Effects on Social Programs

Perhaps one of the biggest ethical questions surrounding the FairTax is whether or not it will undermine the social programs many Americans believe in or depend upon. Many consider the presence of these programs a moral imperative that must be funded by those who are not struggling as much.

While a lot of hoopla has been made about the effects of the FairTax on these programs, it is without any real basis. By design, the FairTax proposal does not include any legislation dealing with the continued existence of Social Security, Medicare, Food Stamps, or any other welfare program. The FairTax is simply meant to be an alternative way of funding these and all other government programs that currently operate under our existing tax system.

That's not to say that politicians won't attempt to eliminate or expand these programs later, but they'll have to do it within the constraints and transparency of the revenue the FairTax generates. Because the FairTax is designed to be revenue neutral (meaning the total amount of tax collected doesn't change), it is hypothetically up to our elected officials to ensure the money needed to fund programs like Social Security continues to make it into the Social Security war chest.

The Least You Need to Know

- Both the current tax system and the FairTax system are progressive, which theoretically shifts the tax burden to people who make or spend the most.

- The current tax system was not the intent of the founding fathers but rather was implemented in 1913 by the Sixteenth Amendment, which the FairTax seeks to overturn.

- The Constitution arguably contains the basis for the government to tax people to fund entitlement programs as well as a protection from anyone being taxed in a discriminatory fashion (the Fourteenth Amendment), both of which the FairTax honors.

- The FairTax legislation does not attempt to make any changes to programs like Social Security, Medicare, or welfare, but rather how the money is collected to fund them.

- Many feel the current tax system seems to unfairly tax business owners who take on much of the risk needed for our economy to grow.

Chapter 9

FairTax Conflicts of Interest

In This Chapter
- Perks of FairTax friendship
- Who are FairTax opponents looking out for?
- Lobbyists and special interest groups
- FairTax fodder for the media

Maybe it's all my years in the financial planning industry or my background in psychotherapy, but I'm a bit of a cynic when it comes to people's intentions. I believe virtually everyone is tempted to act in their own best interest, including politicians and the media. That's not to say that there isn't nobility in the actions people choose or that we shouldn't ever trust people. But rather, when it comes to the decisions we make about our own personal finances and the broader finances of our country, we need to pull back the curtain and see who's flipping the switches (and why).

When it comes to the FairTax, its supporters, and its opponents, there's no doubt that some of the loudest voices have something to gain. This chapter takes a look at who these folks are, without my passing judgment. I'll leave that up to you.

FairTax Supporters with Something to Gain

While the vast majority of supporters have gotten behind the FairTax simply because they're fed up with a system that fails more with every passing year, a few groups of people definitely have something to gain from a switch to the FairTax. I'm not saying that these people are representative of all or even most FairTax supporters, but we should not ignore their influence.

To Be Fair

The politicians voicing support or opposition for the FairTax are no doubt just the tip of the iceberg. As I discovered in a number of interviews in preparation for this book, plenty of politicians on both sides of the aisle love or hate the FairTax. However, many are holding their cards close to the vest until a vote actually takes place, in hopes of not alienating any of their bases before then.

People with Large Estates

Two groups rooting for the FairTax are wealthy Americans and those with significant net worth tied up in a family business who are likely to be hit with the estate tax upon their death. For those unfamiliar with the estate tax, many consider it the tax equivalent of spitting on a dead person's grave.

The estate tax, as well as the gift tax, taxes the transfer of wealth to people besides your spouse, during and after your lifetime. In other words, if you've done a great job of accumulating wealth and paying your fair share of taxes along the way, you may still be hit with an additional federal tax of up to 45 percent after your death. This tax is assessed only if the wealth you leave behind exceeds a certain amount, currently in the ballpark of $1,000,000 per person.

Thus, someone dying with $5,000,000 in wealth (including his real estate holdings) may pay close to $2,000,000 in estate taxes (after 2011). If he happens to leave a large portion of this money to heirs who are more than one generation younger than he, such as his grandchildren, they may be hit with an additional tax known as the generation-skipping tax. This generation-skipping tax can further raise the overall rate that his nonexempt estate is taxed at to above 70 percent.

Of course, under the FairTax the estate tax, gift tax, and generation-skipping tax all disappear. While fans of the FairTax argue this money will eventually be taxed when the heirs spend it, they either don't know about or are ignoring the fact that the FairTax does not tax "used" goods. In other words, the heirs could use their inheritance to purchase used Ferraris and previously owned million-dollar mansions, effectively avoiding taxation on their inheritance.

> **To Be Fair**
>
> The FairTax isn't the only way to get rid of the estate and gift tax system. Under President Bush, the estate tax limit was raised and the tax itself eliminated in 2010. However, that plan actually reinstates the estate tax in the following year (2011), unless Congress takes the highly unlikely step of making the tax cut permanent.

People with Large Retirement Accounts

Aside from their primary residences, the largest asset most Americans own is their 401(k) or other retirement plan accounts such as IRAs. In fact, according to a May 2008 study by the Investment Company Institute (ICI), 40 percent of the financial assets households hold are in these tax-favored retirement plans. The ICI's estimates currently put this amount at over $17 trillion, which is only expected to grow as more and more Americans realize they're on their own when it comes to funding their retirement.

With the exception of Roth IRAs, the vast majority of these assets have never been taxed. This is the result of the government trying to encourage personal savings by allowing amounts contributed to retirement plans to be subtracted from the income reported on W-2 and tax returns. The wrinkle, of course, is that this money is eventually supposed

to be taxed at ordinary income tax rates when it's
withdrawn.

For someone with a $250,000 or $500,000 account
balance (which is very common for a 40- to 50-year-
old, even in a lousy economy), this may mean that
with the FairTax they would effectively avoid paying
tens of thousands, or even hundreds of thousands, of
dollars in income tax.

People with Money Offshore

As talked about in Chapter 6, one of the most
legitimate economic boons to be gained from
the FairTax is that Americans may move back on
shore money they've held in *offshore bank accounts*.
While some people and companies holding this
money in places like the Cayman Islands or in Swiss
bank accounts have done so through legal means,
many have transferred the money illegally to avoid
income taxation. In fact, as I write this book, one of
the largest investment firms in the United States is
being investigated by the U.S. government for its
role in helping over 50,000 wealthy Americans illegally move assets offshore.

The passage of the FairTax would allow these
otherwise normal Americans, who have engaged in
a criminal activity to shield their assets from taxes
and lawsuits, to slowly move these assets back on
shore and reduce their risk of ending up in jail.
Considering the increased amount of scrutiny fall-
ing on these tax cheats, there's no doubt that many
would like to see the FairTax enacted so they can

earn a tax-free rate of return in a less felonious manner.

def•i•ni•tion

Offshore bank accounts are accounts whose earnings are shielded from U.S. reporting laws, meaning that the interest and investment growth in the account is invisible to the IRS. While some corporations may legally move their operations offshore, individual citizens are not permitted to do so for purposes of tax evasion.

People with Low Consumption

Since the FairTax is a consumption-based national sales tax, it would affect people only to the extent that they spend. So a couple who earns $250,000 but only spends $50,000 per year will pay less in taxes than a couple who earns $60,000 and spends every dime of it. This naturally means that people who already have their major expenses taken care of (they've paid off their home, raised their kids, etc.), would likely spend less than someone who is still working toward these major expenses.

Business Owners, Corporations, and Shareholders

One of the biggest beneficiaries of the FairTax will no doubt be the business community. Most FairTax fans acknowledge this as one of the prime perks of the system, which they hope will also result in more jobs, business growth, etc. Of course, that doesn't mean everyone benefits equally.

While not all corporations are taxed (such as sub-chapter S corporations), many are hit with a tax rate in the ballpark of 35 percent. This means that 35 percent of the net profit (after they pay their employees and other costs) goes back to Uncle Sam. In theory, that's 35 percent they could plow back into the business or into hiring new employees. Of course, it's also 35 percent they could use in part to increase the compensation of their company's exec-utives, who have become known for their already outrageous compensation packages that oftentimes seem to go well beyond economic reason.

Employers, whether they're the larger corporations just mentioned or small businesses with only a few employees, definitely have something to gain if the FairTax eliminates their payroll-related taxes. Keep in mind that your employer matches your Social Security and Medicare contributions at a rate of 7.65 percent of every dollar you earn. That means that small businesses with $200,000 in annual pay-roll currently have to pay an additional $15,300 in FICA taxes on top of that cost.

These additional FICA taxes are even more pain-ful for small businesses where the owner is also the only employee. In these situations, he pays both sides of the FICA contribution, or 15.3 percent—which actually drops to 13.6 percent due to self-employment deduction. So you Joe the Plumbers of the world who make $50,000 per year pay $7,650 in FICA taxes alone, and that's before you pay any income tax or other disability taxes.

Your Wallet

Some business people rooting for the FairTax are under the mistaken impression that it would eliminate their workers' compensation costs in addition to their other payroll costs. Unfortunately, individual states generally administer workers' compensation, so the introduction of the FairTax would not likely affect it.

It is worth mentioning that anything made above the Social Security wage base, which was $106,800 in 2009, goes untaxed for Social Security purposes. Unfortunately, there is no cap on the Medicare portion of the FICA calculation, which still amounts to 2.9 percent annually.

FairTax Opponents with Something to Lose

Like many who are for the FairTax, most who oppose it do so strictly on a gut level. From what few details they've heard or read, they've decided they don't like it or don't trust those pushing it. Many of these people don't fully understand it, or they'd probably be more open to the discussion, even if still cautious.

But also like those who favor the FairTax, there is a small but vocal portion of opponents who are, in this case, working their hardest to talk people out of it. For these people, it's not so much that they think it'll be bad for the country as much as they think it'll be bad for them. Just like the minority who has a lot to gain under the FairTax, we need to take the opinions of those with a lot to lose with a grain of salt.

Currently Untaxed Service Industries

One group that is shaking in its boots over the FairTax is service professionals. For the most part, the services you and I purchase from these people are not subject to a sales tax of any kind, unlike products or merchandise we might buy that are often taxed by individual states.

Your Wallet

People with large "service" expenses that were previously deductible may suffer under the FairTax. For example, retirees who pay no payroll taxes and have $10,000 per year in deductible medical expenses would likely only pay between $6,500 and $9,000 for these expenses after deducting this on their federal tax return under the current system. If this amount ceases to be deductible and the price of the service with the FairTax added remains roughly the same, these individuals will likely see their overall out-of-pocket costs increase.

Currently, people who charge $100 per hour for their advice or $50 an hour for their labor know most of us cringe as we write the check or swipe our card. Often, many of us feel like these professionals are ripping us off because they're the only ones who can provide the services we need. Naturally, the idea of having to add a 23 percent sales tax to those costs would force business owners to choose between having to answer to irate customers or reducing their prices, neither of which is a discussion that these people would like to have.

As mentioned previously in the discussion of embedded taxation (see Chapter 3), service professionals' worries may not be unfounded. Since their primary product is their time, they may carry less of an embedded tax in their pricing than someone whose product is manufactured and relies on raw materials that carry significant embedded taxes. Thus, whereas many retailers' costs would drop, making up for the presence of the FairTax, many service professionals may simply have their larger margins squeezed downward.

The Tax Preparation Industry

To lump all accountants together as a group and say they're either opposed to or in favor of the FairTax would be inaccurate. Some say accountants love the FairTax because it would free them up to focus on more profitable activities, while others say accountants are holding on to the current system for dear life.

While it's true that a substantial number of Certified Public or Certified Management Accountants (CPAs or CMAs) would refocus on more profitable activities under the FairTax, it's only true to the extent that their practice is not built around preparing taxes. In fact, most of the accountants I know from my experience in the financial services industry only do taxes. They have no interest in helping businesses do their day-to-day accounting or making financial decisions. These folks make a great six-figure living working a small portion of the year doing individual tax returns. Not surprisingly, most within this group are very opposed to the idea of the overnight death of the tax preparation industry.

Further, there are just as many "nonaccountant" professionals, whether they are state-certified tax preparers or Enrolled Agents, who make their living primarily off the preparation of taxes. Many of these folks are less than excited about having to learn a new career in their mid-40s or 50s.

Lobbyists and Special Interest Groups

While it may not dawn on most people initially, scoring a tax deduction for a certain type of expense can fuel an entire industry. One need look no further than the real estate industry and real estate agents, who benefit from the fact that many Americans believe they should buy a home to "get the deduction."

Passage of the FairTax would essentially level the playing field between different classes of deductible and nondeductible expenses, as well as between tax-favored and average businesses. This in turn would essentially rob lobbyists and special interest groups of their ability to push their agendas with tax deductions as the primary tool. Still, as previously mentioned, politicians have some ability to reward their home states and congressional districts, due to the fact that those who collect the FairTax get to keep a small portion of it.

The Media, the FairTax, and Grassroots Organizations

If you've read any of my other books, especially *The Complete Idiot's Guide to Boosting Your Financial IQ,* you know that I'm first in line to bash my own industry. The professional media is a capitalist industry like any other and should always be viewed as such. Whether it's the evening news, talk radio, or the publishing industry, we're all in it to make a living. Not surprisingly, the best livings are often made by those who do a good job at grabbing attention and telling their audience what they want to hear.

With that in mind, don't take anything you read, hear, or watch for an undisputable fact or as the sole answer to your questions. Whether it's this or other books about the FairTax, sound bites on the evening news, or especially commercials aired by those for or against it, continue to take the initiative of doing your own homework.

Likewise, be careful about regurgitating things you find in online chat rooms, either for or against the FairTax, without verifying the information. I've been lurking around these chat rooms for months in preparation for writing this book and can promise you that much of what you read in these forums is like a really bad version of that old game of "telephone." Passionate people with good intentions continue to pass on evolving misinformation that looks less and less like the FairTax proposal or the legitimate arguments for or against it.

One thing's for sure—as the FairTax continues to gather steam, which I believe it will, you'll hear more and more so-called "facts" about it. Wonderfully, though, the FairTax proposal is a relatively short read, and many of the conclusions themselves are common sense. At the end of this book you'll find Appendix B, which contains links to a variety of websites and resources where you can verify the information you find in this book and elsewhere for yourself.

The Least You Need to Know

- There's no doubt that the FairTax creates some sizeable loopholes for wealthy households to avoid income and estate taxation.
- Lobbyists and special interest groups would love to keep the current tax system since it lets them use tax deductions to promote their industries.

- Untaxed service industries, whose products come with very little embedded taxation, may feel a FairTax pinch more than retailers.

- Employers will undoubtedly benefit under the FairTax, but it's not guaranteed that they'll pass all this benefit on to the consumer.

- The media loves a circus, and there's no doubt that the FairTax debate is becoming one. To make an informed decision, do your homework!

10

Alternatives to the FairTax

In This Chapter

- A brief history of U.S. taxes
- Fixing the current system
- The surprisingly popular flat tax
- The value-added tax—Europe's choice

While the FairTax may seem like the near-perfect solution to many, we would be careless not to consider all the alternatives. Choosing the FairTax just because it seems better than the current system would be the wrong choice if another, better alternative went unchosen. Unfortunately, many of those strongly for or against the FairTax can't accurately sum up how our current system works, much less explain the other alternatives.

Thus, a key in evaluating the FairTax is recognizing how it differs from the other proposals for reform. In fact, at any given time we can almost guarantee that someone in the House of Representatives or the Senate is trying to garner support for some type of tax reform, be it changes to our current system or a replacement system altogether. To get you up to speed, let's take a look at the history of taxation in the United States as well as the three most popular alternatives outside the FairTax.

A Brief History of Taxes

Perhaps nothing is more valuable in evaluating alternative tax systems than a healthy understanding of what's already been tried. It surprises many to know that the United States has already tried a number of tax systems ranging from extensive excise taxes (on everything from chewing gum to pianos), to a flat tax, to a personal income tax rate that reached as high as 94 percent!

Tariffs and Excise Taxes

In both colonial America and for a number of years after the United States was founded, the primary sources of tax revenue were *tariffs* imposed on imports and exports, excise taxes on the sale of certain goods, and real estate taxes. Taxes such as these, imposed under the Stamp Act and the Tea Act, led to the cries of "no taxation without representation," the Boston Tea Party (the great-grandfather of today's Tea Party movement), and eventually the Revolutionary War with England.

After the colonies won their independence from England, these taxes continued, albeit with better political representation for those the taxes were levied upon. In fact, to help pay for the Revolutionary War and the cost of a new nation, the number of these taxes increased, leading to excise taxes on a wide variety of other items. Many of these new taxes led to violent, armed rebellions by U.S. citizens against the government, including the Whiskey Rebellion, Shays Rebellion, and Fries Rebellion.

def•i•ni•tion

> A **tariff** is a tax imposed on imported goods from other countries. Many countries enter into tax treaties with the United States so that their exports sent here and vice versa are not subject to tariffs.

Relative to the proposed FairTax, we should note its similarity to the broad use of excise taxes in the earliest days of America. First, although these excise taxes were not a uniformly applied sales tax such as the FairTax, they were a tax nonetheless imposed on the purchase of certain goods. This imposition of taxes was not well-received by all citizens (to the point of armed rebellions), and we should accept the possibility that not all Americans will receive a confusing 23 percent inclusive national sales tax with open arms. It wouldn't be surprising if passage of the FairTax is a catalyst for as many "tea parties" as it puts an end to.

Second, considering that the current excise taxes that exist in the United States will not necessarily end under the FairTax, it's possible that some producers and manufacturers of goods will feel that a 23 percent sales tax on top of already high excise taxes unfairly punishes their industries.

The Introduction of Income Taxes

After a four-decade period in the 1800s during which most taxes were completely suspended, the government embarked on a period of heavy taxation in 1861 to fund the Civil War. Not only did Congress introduce excise taxes on random items such as feathers and pianos, it also introduced the first true income tax at this point.

> ### To Be Fair
>
> While many people are quick to dismiss antitax supporters who advocate eliminating income taxes altogether, note that the United States has spent more than half of its existence (130 years) without an income tax.

Under the income tax introduced in 1861, all yearly income over $800 (or $21,541 in 2009, adjusted for 2.25 percent annual inflation) was taxed at a rate of 3 percent. This system lasted for one year, and then was replaced by a progressive bracket system, which taxed no income below $600. Income earned between $600 and $10,000 was taxed at 3 percent, with income above $10,000 taxed at 5 percent. This tax system of 1862 also introduced employer withholding to ensure collection and cut down on tax avoidance.

After 10 more years, this income tax system was abolished in 1872 due to a drop-off in the government's revenue needs, with adequate revenue being collected from excise taxes alone. Aside from an attempt to institute a flat income tax near the end of the 1800s, which was quickly ruled unconstitutional because it was not apportioned among the states based on population, no income tax was charged again until 1913.

Following the passage of the Sixteenth Amendment to the U.S. Constitution in 1913, which allowed the federal government to impose taxes directly on citizens without apportioning it fairly based on state population, the modern progressive income tax was instituted once and for all. The rates under this first tax system ranged from as low as 1 percent to over 7 percent, with most Americans effectively avoiding any taxation whatsoever due to the high exemption level on income (the first $3,000 in income went untaxed, or roughly $32,000 in today's dollars).

Your Wallet

During the Great Depression, President Franklin Roosevelt introduced Social Security payroll taxes, which for many Americans is the single largest tax they pay. The first payroll deductions began in 1937.

The decades that followed saw income tax rates on a roller coaster ride, with the top rate raised as high as 73 percent to fund World War I, dropped as low as 25 percent during the roaring 1920s, and then hiked as high as 79 percent during the Great Depression. In the years immediately following

World War II, Americans saw the rate hiked as high as 94 percent, with it leveling off at 91 percent in the early 1960s. From the 1970s on, the top tax rate gradually began to slide, dropping as low as 28 percent in 1988 and stabilizing in the mid to upper 30 percent range through the end of the century.

Starting under President Reagan, tax reform moved to the forefront of many political discussions and campaigns, with politicians and presidents using changes to the tax codes to stimulate the economy and encourage personal savings and investments.

Alternative #1: Fix the Current System

While some are ready to throw in the towel on the current tax system, others argue that it's not as bad as it seems. Rather, they believe it can be repaired with much less work than switching to the FairTax or another system.

Believers in the current tax system assert that many of the primary concerns, such as the tax code's complexity, embedded taxes, and audit procedures, can be dealt with simply. Further, they argue that the tax system doesn't cost most Americans as much as antitax advocates would have us believe. Of course, the one thing that we cannot address, no matter how much the current system is tweaked, is its progressive nature that penalizes higher-income earners more than those with less income.

To make the current system competitive with what the FairTax seeks to accomplish, the following would need to happen:

- **Lower individual and corporate rates—** Much of the FairTax's hypothetical magic comes from the removal of embedded taxes in the cost of goods and services. To accomplish this under the current system, we must substantially reduce tax rates, especially those of corporations that are essentially taxed twice.

- **Provide alternative funding for entitlement programs—**Since the employer contribution to Social Security and Medicare is a major source of embedded taxes, as well as the employee's contribution from his paycheck, we would need to create an alternative funding mechanism.

Look It Up

Before we can think about changing the current system, we need to get a handle on who pays what, the most popular deductions, etc. One of the best places to begin searching for this information is found right on the IRS's website at www.irs.gov/taxstats.

- **Remove limitations on deductions—**Many of the juiciest deductions in the tax code are phased out for households that earn too much. To create a more fair and equitable tax system, we must make the same deductions available to all taxpayers.

- **End vote-buying deductions**—Many of the deductions in place cater to special interest groups and certain voter bases. We need to remove these as well as add deductions for things like renting (not just buying) a home.

- **Create an export rebate**—One of the FairTax's strongest economic contributions would be the removal of embedded taxes from American goods prior to sale in the global markets. By creating an export tax rebate where businesses have their taxes lowered based on their level of exports, they could pass this savings on to the global market and increase their competitiveness.

- **Eliminate the estate, gift, and alternative minimum taxes**—Taxing Americans a second time upon their death (through estate and gift taxes) or because they have too many otherwise legitimate deductions (the alternative minimum tax) seems to be the exact opposite of fair. Considering that these taxes, especially the estate tax, collect only a small portion of the nation's total revenue, it may be time for them to go.

- **Revamp IRS audit procedures**—FairTaxers aren't the only people with a well-founded disdain and fear of the IRS. By revamping the audit selection procedures to better reflect our constitutional rights, the current tax code would become less heinous to many.

Alternative #2: The Flat Tax

If any one tax alternative has grabbed a lot of attention, it's the flat tax concept, where all Americans supposedly pay the same flat tax rate on their income. In fact, modern-day flat tax proposals have received more support in Congress than the FairTax. One of the most recent versions of the flat tax, The Taxpayer Choice Act of 2007 (which many would argue is not a true flat tax because it had two rates—10 percent and 25 percent), received 90 co-sponsors in the House of Representatives.

Look It Up

If you're interested in learning more about recent flat tax proposals, visit http://thomas.loc.gov and search for bill "H.R. 3818." You can also find more information at www.scrapthecode.org, a website run by the nonprofit organization FreedomWorks.

A number of high-level politicians, including former House Majority Leader Dick Armey, presidential candidate Fred Thompson, and presidential candidate Steve Forbes, have also endorsed flat tax proposals. Adding even more legitimacy to the flat tax concept is the fact that the United States previously used it for the federal tax system, and 8 states and over 20 other countries currently use it.

> **To Be Fair**
>
> The states currently using a flat income tax rate include Colorado, Hawaii, Illinois, Massachusetts, Pennsylvania, and Utah. Countries currently using a flat income tax system include Russia, Iceland, the Czech Republic, and Iraq.

Despite all its fans, flat tax critics would tell you, correctly, that most of these proposals are not as flat as they look. Most flat tax proposals still come with deductions that favor certain expenditures and income exemptions, which can make it look more like a set of stairs than a flat tax. FairTax fans would also argue that the flat tax is also still ultimately an income tax, which carries with it a variety of economy-stifling characteristics.

Alternative #3: The Value-Added Tax (VAT)

If the question of how other industrialized nations tax their population hasn't crossed your mind, it should. Naturally, before we ditch our entire tax code and start from scratch designing a new one, we may want to look at other established systems.

When we do take a look around, we see that roughly two thirds of the countries in the world, and virtually every other industrialized nation, uses what is known as a value-added tax (VAT) to collect some or all of their revenues. In fact, a number of countries actually use the VAT in addition to a personal income tax.

The VAT, like the FairTax, is essentially a national sales tax. Unlike the FairTax, however, it's not paid only by the end-consumer at the time of purchase. It's actually paid by each vendor or manufacturer along the way as it moves to market. The amount of the VAT actually remitted to the government by each party is simply the difference between the VAT they paid acquiring it and the VAT collected when they sold it to the next business.

For example, let's say that an auto parts business bought a radiator for $50 and the national VAT rate is 15 percent. The total price the auto parts business pays to the radiator manufacturing company is $57.50 ($50 plus $7.50 in VAT).

Now, when the auto parts store sells the radiator for $60, they'd also collect a VAT of $9 ($60 × 15 percent) for a grand total of $69. But since they already paid a VAT of $7.50 to buy the radiator, they would only have to submit $1.50 to the government, or the difference between the VAT they paid and the VAT they collected. Another way of looking at it is that the VAT they will owe is the VAT rate multiplied by their markup on the pre-VAT price of the item ($10 markup × 15 percent VAT = $1.50).

Your Wallet

If you're planning to travel to any of the European countries such as the United Kingdom or France, or other locales that charge the VAT, be sure to do your homework on the possibility of receiving a VAT rebate. Many countries that use the VAT offer a rebate on the money that tourists spend in their country. More information about VAT refunds can be found in most online travel guides such as GoEurope. About.com.

If this sounds like more work than a traditional sales tax or the FairTax, you're right. But there are a number of key benefits that VAT advocates like to point out:

- **Harder to evade**—With a traditional sales tax such as the FairTax, where intermediate purchases by businesses are exempt from taxation, the only point of collection is when the consumer buys the goods. Thus, if that one business fails to collect the tax, the revenue is lost. Because the VAT is collected at each stage of production, it arguably has a lower rate of potential avoidance than the FairTax or personal income taxes.

- **Rebates for exports**—Many nations that use the VAT allow a rebate for the VAT on exported items. This can remove some or all of the embedded taxes (depending on if a country also charges an income tax), making the exported good or service more competitive in foreign markets, similar to the FairTax.

- **Possible elimination of individual taxes**— Depending on the rate collected under a VAT system, a country could hypothetically do away with income taxes. This would accomplish many of the same simplification goals attained under the FairTax.

- **Multiple rates**—A VAT system, unlike the FairTax proposal, offers different rates for certain items. Generally a VAT system will have a full VAT rate, a reduced rate, and a "zero" rate. The lower rates are used for certain necessity and nonluxury items. Some argue that this would be a more accurate way of making sure the poor are not overtaxed, instead of simply handing out money indiscriminately like the FairTax prebate.

Of course, that's not to say that the VAT doesn't have its shortfalls—namely, the amount of additional time that goes into tracking what a business has paid and collected under the VAT system. But VAT advocates argue that the difference between this and the monthly calculations required under the FairTax are negligible.

The Least You Need to Know

- Early America did not rely on a personal income tax; instead it taxed the purchases of selected items.

- FairTax advocates should not overlook reform of the current system as a potential middle ground in their fight for more fair and efficient taxation.

- The flat tax has a long history in both the United States and around the world, with a strong renewed interest in recent years.

- Over half the world's countries use the value-added tax (VAT), which is a legitimate contender against the FairTax if the United States pursues a national sales tax system.

Chapter 11

What's Next for the FairTax

In This Chapter

- Reading the FairTax proposal
- Making a decision for yourself
- The FairTax transition
- Expanding your knowledge

Chances are that everything you've read so far leaves you at a crossroads when it comes to the FairTax. There's probably part of you that thinks this proposal could really be all that it's cracked up to be, and part of you that has a knee-jerk reaction to the idea of a 23 percent (or possibly more) non-negotiable national sales tax. If you find yourself at that crossroads, I have just one thing to say—*good!*

In reality, the FairTax, while relatively simple in its design, is not nearly as simple in its guaranteed effects. While people on both sides of the argument would have you believe their argument for or against the FairTax is black and white, it's just not that neat and tidy. *Reality check—we're talking about completely revamping the way the most powerful nation in the world refills its economic gas tank!*

So from here, my goal for you is not so much to make a decision for or against the FairTax, but rather a decision to keep investigating it.

Questions That Need Answering

As you further evaluate the FairTax proposal, I want to give you a roadmap for asking the questions that will probably matter the most. In asking these, I encourage you to look out for not only your own financial interests (the obvious ones), but also those of the people with more and less money than you. You're ultimately trying to find a system that is both fair and productive—one that doesn't penalize people for having too much or too little money, while simultaneously contributing to the overall health of economy.

- **Which system is more fair?** Does our current system or the proposed FairTax system penalize people for making too much money? Does it penalize those who have fallen on hard times? Similarly, does either give unfair breaks to those who have made it to the top or encourage those at the bottom to stay put?

- **How will it affect your wallet?** In the end, will the FairTax cost you more, less, or the same as it does now? What would happen if you lose your job or get a promotion? Or if your expenditures climb or decrease due to changes in your family or lifestyle? Do you think the increase in take-home pay would be enough to offset a possible increase in prices?

Your Wallet

It'll be hard to evaluate the FairTax's effect on your wallet if you don't have a good handle on what taxes cost you under the current system. Before you go any further, pull out your last few years' IRS Form 1040s and take a look at the line that says "This is your total tax." Divide your total income by this number, add 7.65 percent, and you'll get a real number that you can compare against the 23 percent FairTax.

- **How will it affect prices?** Will prices increase 23 percent or more as some fear? Will they stay the same or go down as some people promise? Will they be somewhere in between? Will the goods and services you rely on be affected more or less than what others use?

- **How will it affect the economy?** To be a rich man in a dying economy is not a cheery scenario, so you need to weigh the broad effects, not just your own pocketbook. Will it really spur the economy as people promise, or will it do the opposite? Will it save programs like Social Security and Medicare, or is the current system the best bet? How will it affect international trade, imports, exports, and tourism?

- **What do its strongest opponents/ advocates have to gain or lose?** We should be fair and admit that few, if any, of us are free from our own self-interest, political biases, etc. But what about those people who are championing the cause for or against the FairTax—what do they have to gain? Are they trying to sell books, please their constituents, or simply be a voice of opposition to the way things are? Or do they really, whole-heartedly believe in their vote for or against the FairTax?

Reading the FairTax Proposal

All I can say is, "Don't be that person." You know, the one who has all kinds of opinions one way or another about the FairTax but hasn't actually read the legislation. Online message boards, forwarded e-mails, and talking points from your favorite (or least favorite) politician are no substitute for knowing what the FairTax proposal actually says.

Thankfully, reading the entire FairTax proposal takes just a couple lazy hours over the weekend or a few lunch breaks at work. I'd suggest you read it with a highlighter and pen in hand so you can identify things of importance, as well as write down questions you want to come back and investigate later.

For the record, the FairTax Act in the House of Representatives and the FairTax Act in the Senate are identical, so it doesn't matter which one you read. To help you navigate the bill, here's a section-by-section breakdown of the FairTax proposal:

Look It Up

Since copies of the FairTax legislation aren't sold at your local bookstore, you'll need to look it up online. Visit the Library of Congress at http://thomas.loc.gov and search for "Fair Tax." Be sure the copy you're looking at is the most recent.

- **Section 1**—This first page of the FairTax Act contains the table of contents for the entire bill. If you can't find something, this is the place to start looking.

- **Section 2, Congressional Findings**—This section is a little confusing for first-time readers since it talks about agreed-upon "Congressional Findings." Someone reading this might wonder how, if everyone agrees that everything listed here is true, they haven't already enacted the FairTax. Well, despite what people may say, Congress hasn't agreed on everything in this section. It's actually meant to reflect what they believe Congress would say should they pass this bill. The opinions in this section are nowhere close to unanimous.

- **Title I, Repeal of Taxes**—This portion of the FairTax bill repeals (eliminates) the federal income tax, estate and gift taxes, and payroll taxes relating to Social Security and Medicare. It also sets the date the FairTax, if passed, would go into effect.

- **Title II, The Sales Tax (FairTax) Enacted**—The primary purpose of this section is to set the FairTax rate (Title II, Ch. 1), define the exemptions and credits (Title II, Ch. 2), set the monthly prebate (Title II, Ch. 3), define the role of businesses and states in collecting the tax (Title II, Ch. 4), and set the special rules for things like gambling and nonprofit organizations (Title II, Ch. 7). The beginning of this section also contains a number of key definitions used throughout the rest of the bill.

- **Title III, Phase-Out of Repealed Federal Taxes**—This section primarily highlights the changeover process from the current IRS-driven system to the FairTax.

- **Title IV, Possible Sunset (Cancellation) of FairTax**—This short section contains a *sunset clause* that basically repeals the FairTax if the Sixteenth Amendment of the Constitution is not also repealed within seven years of the FairTax being passed. This is to essentially protect Americans from the risk of double-taxation (both a sales tax and an income tax).

def•i•ni•tion

Sunset clauses found in certain laws create a date in the future at which that law will cease to exist. It's essentially used to create temporary laws that depend on a vote or certain conditions in order to be renewed.

What's Next for the FairTax?

While the FairTax seems to have huge grassroots support (FairTax.org claims 800,000 "members"), it's still a long way from becoming the law of the land. A number of key things need to fall into place in order for this to happen.

First and foremost, both the Senate and the House of Representatives need to approve the FairTax Act. In both houses of Congress, this generally requires the bill to make its way through a preliminary committee and then be approved by a simple majority vote.

From there, the FairTax would be put on the president's desk for his signature. Of course, the president can use his veto power to keep the bill from becoming a law. If this were the case, a two-thirds majority vote of the combined Congress (the House of Representatives and the Senate) could overrule the veto.

Of course, a presidential signature or Congress overriding a veto wouldn't even ensure the FairTax is here to stay. That's because the last section of the FairTax legislation requires the Sixteenth Amendment of the Constitution to be repealed within seven years, or the FairTax itself will expire. For this to happen, three fourths of the state legislatures would have to vote in favor of repealing the Sixteenth Amendment.

How likely is all this to happen in the next few years? All signs point to "not very likely." Though there are claims that the FairTax has bipartisan support, it's minimal at best. Considering the recent shift of the political axis toward the left and the Democratic Party, it's unlikely that a primarily Republican-led tax overhaul will be given much attention in the corridors of power in the near future. This seems especially true as the far-right Conservative movement often most visibly advocates the bill.

> **To Be Fair**
>
> While some people might consider it a fantasy that three fourths of the states would stand behind the FairTax, remember that that is exactly how the Sixteenth Amendment, which granted broad taxation powers, came into being fewer than 100 years ago.

Does this mean the discussion is dead and has no hope? Not at all. Rather, it means that those who believe in the FairTax need to continue to educate themselves so they can educate others about how the FairTax works and its possible benefits and limitations.

If the FairTax Passes ...

What would the U.S. tax system look like in the weeks and months following the passage of the FairTax? The day after the FairTax actually passed a vote, the only thing that would noticeably change would be the look on most Americans' faces. It'd likely be a mix of excitement, confusion, hope, and impending doom. As far as it actually hitting people's pocketbooks, that would take a little longer.

In each *congressional term*, when the FairTax is reintroduced, a new date is set for a hypothetically approved FairTax to go into effect. Under the FairTax Act of 2009, the effective date (when you'd start getting charged the FairTax) is January 1, 2011. If the FairTax does not get approved in this congressional cycle, it will likely get reintroduced with a new date a few years into the future.

def•i•ni•tion

> **Congressional terms** consist of two year-long sessions. A bill such as the FairTax Act is often reintroduced at the beginning of each two-year congressional term as its authors attempt to rally an increasing level of support.

On the date set in the agreement, businesses and states would begin collecting the FairTax and remitting it to the U.S. Treasury. Also beginning on this date, paychecks would no longer show deductions for federal income tax withholding, FICA (OASDI) insurance, or Medicare (hospital insurance).

The Slow Death of the IRS

In a FairTax world, the IRS would be slowly phased out over a couple years. This would mean that almost immediately, the IRS would begin laying off staff devoted to long-term projects and low-revenue operations such as literature creation.

For the remainder of its short life, the IRS's focus would likely shift to audits with a high probability of payoff, investigating abusive tax shelters, and resolving open cases and outstanding balances. At the same time, the government and the IRS would begin downsizing their huge infrastructure, especially in the real estate department.

After two years, according to the current FairTax legislation, the IRS as we know it would cease to exist and taxpayer records would be destroyed. Some of the few remaining IRS employees would possibly transfer over to help administer and oversee the FairTax as part of the new Department of Treasury Sales Tax Bureau or one of the other smaller offices the FairTax Act creates.

The FairTax Changeover for Businesses

One of the biggest concerns brought up about a transition to the FairTax system is the treatment of a business's existing inventory that already has embedded taxes in it. If businesses were forced to charge the FairTax on top of the taxes that were already embedded in those items when purchased, they'd either lose customers or money.

The FairTax Act takes this into account, allowing a business a Transitional Inventory Credit on goods sold before the end of the FairTax's first year in existence. This credit is calculated by multiplying the business's cost of purchasing that inventory by the FairTax rate (expected to be 23 percent).

> **To Be Fair**
>
> Perhaps it'd be more accurate to say that a FairTax changeover would be relatively painless for most industries. There is, of course, a huge industry built around our tax system, from preparers to software manufactures to financial publications. Companies and experts in these industries will have to figure out a way to diversify and retool or face extinction.

Another concern is the retooling of cash registers to account for the sales tax. However, since most cash registers are now electronic and easily reprogrammable, the adjustment for most businesses at the point of sale will be relatively painless if noticed at all.

The FairTax Changeover for the Consumer

The changeover to the FairTax for the consumer may run the spectrum from relatively painless to nightmarish, depending on a couple possible scenarios. In the least painful scenario, some individuals who get paid at the end of December and still have income and payroll taxes withheld may find themselves coming up slightly short in January when some or all of their goods have increased in price. Of course, their next paycheck will increase without any federal income or payroll taxes withheld from it, and prices will have likely stabilized, meaning their discomfort was temporary at best.

In a worst-case scenario, prices would not drop as quickly or at all, as predicted by FairTax opposers. Expenses such as home rental rates, cell phone plans, and other contractual obligations would jump in cost, leaving lower-income consumers who paid no tax anyway under the current system scrambling to break contracts, find new living arrangements, etc.

To add insult to injury is the possibility that individual states, many of which have found themselves teetering on bankruptcy in recent years, see the disappearance of a federal income tax as an opportunity to raise their own state income taxes—something that's well within their rights.

On a positive note, however, most taxpayers would no longer have to worry about saving receipts, tracking mileage, buying tax preparation software, or fretting over questionable or confusing deductions. Administratively, their lives would become immeasurably easier the day the FairTax goes into effect.

Getting More Involved With the FairTax

If there's one thing the FairTax is not, it's ignorable. Support for it on Main Street in America is spreading like wildfire. Support for it, or at least a serious and definitive discussion about it, is growing in Washington's corridors of power. There's no chance it will just fade away, and it's just a matter of time before you or your duly elected representative is asked to make a choice about it.

So whether you need to do more research or you've made a decision and are ready to take a stand on either side, it's in your country's best interest that you get moving. In doing so, here's a list of resources that I suggest you give a look:

- **FairTaxGuide.com**—The companion website for this book is chock-full of articles, links, and interactive discussion groups. It's a great place to stay up-to-date on the progress of the FairTax, ask questions as they arise, and partake in a little spirited discussion.

- **Contact your elected officials**—It's crucial that you let your elected officials know where you stand on the FairTax proposal. Visit www.congress.org and type in your zip code to find e-mail links for your senators and representatives.

- **Books by Neal Boortz**—This conservative radio host minces no words—he's in love with the FairTax. Whether you've fallen for it, too, or just want to hear a perspective from the other side, check out Neal's two "love letters" to the FairTax.

- ***The FairTax Fantasy* by Hank Adler and Hugh Hewitt**—Before you think all conservatives are gaga over the FairTax, you've got to check out this book by conservative radio host Hugh Hewitt.

- **FairTax.org**—One of the best entry points for people wanting to learn more about the FairTax or find a local pro-FairTax group is the official website for the Americans for Fair Taxation. You can find research papers (all in favor of the FairTax) and all kinds of other info here.

The Least You Need to Know

- Adopting the FairTax has gigantic ramifications for your family and future generations—it's your job to ask the hard questions!

- Before you do anything else, spend the two or three hours it takes to read the entire FairTax proposal.

- For the FairTax to become law, its supporters will have to move mountains and convince both the majority of Congress and the President of the United States.

- Once you make a decision on where you stand with the FairTax, contact your elected official and make your opinion known!

Appendix A

Glossary

alternative minimum tax (AMT) An existing U.S. income tax system meant to tax higher-income individuals who otherwise escape taxation. Not all higher-income individuals are subject to the AMT, only those who utilize certain deductions and receive certain types of income.

capital gains tax An alternative and lower tax rate charged on assets (stocks, bonds, real estate, etc.) sold for a profit that have also met certain requirements for length of ownership.

consumption tax A tax consumers, but not manufacturers, usually pay on purchases. In its simplest definition, the FairTax is a consumption tax.

embedded tax The increase in the price of goods to account for taxes paid by the manufacturer or retailer, including corporate income taxes and payroll taxes.

estate tax A tax assessed on the wealth transferred to nonspousal persons, above and beyond certain basic exemption amounts.

excise tax   A tax often placed on certain industries that are thought to contribute a greater overall cost to society.

exclusive tax   A tax added on top of the price of the item you buy.

Federal Insurance Contribution Act (FICA) A payroll tax levied against both employees and their employers to fund the Medicare and Social Security programs.

flat tax system   An income tax system whose rate remains the same regardless of how much money an individual makes.

general welfare clause   Wording in the U.S. Constitution that permits the government to collect taxes to provide for the public defense and public welfare.

generation-skipping tax   An additional estate tax charged if a certain amount of inherited assets "skip" more than one generation (i.e., from grandparent to grandchild).

gift tax   A tax, assessed in coordination with the estate tax, on amounts given to another (nonspouse) individual in excess of the IRS annual limit.

inclusive tax   A tax included in the price of the item you buy.

income tax bracket   The rate at which certain unique levels of income are taxed separately from other portions of one's income.

offshore money   Money held in accounts not subject to U.S. reporting requirements, used by corporations and individuals to shield their investments and businesses from ongoing taxation.

prebate   A monthly amount refunded to every taxpayer under the FairTax plan meant to cover the FairTax paid on someone's monthly living expenses up to the current federal poverty line.

progressive tax system   A tax system whose rate increases on individuals' increased incremental income as it exceeds certain levels.

regressive tax system   A tax system whose rate decreases on individuals' increased incremental income as it drops below certain levels.

S corporation   A special kind of corporation designed to give small business owners the ability to incorporate, with profits being passed through to the owners and taxed only at their income tax bracket.

Self-Employed Contribution Act (SECA)
The self-employed person's version of the FICA program, used to fund Medicare and Social Security programs. The rates charged under SECA are identical to FICA.

shadow economy   The national total of income hidden or not reported to the IRS because the transactions are illegal or because certain taxpayers wish to avoid taxation on otherwise legal activities.

special interest groups   Groups that exert influence on politicians to craft laws that favor certain industries.

tax compliance   The process of determining an individual's tax liability, reporting it, and paying any balances owed. It is often talked about in terms of the costs to achieve tax compliance on an individual and collective level.

tax credit   A subtraction directly from the amount of tax owed by someone, which is typically more valuable than a tax deduction.

tax deduction   A subtraction made against someone's income prior to the amount of tax owed being calculated on that income.

value-added tax (VAT)   A tax levied on goods at each stage of their production, from raw materials to the finished product. While there are some similarities between the pricing of VAT-taxed goods and FairTax goods, they are not the same type of tax.

vote buying   The political tactic of promising tax breaks to certain classes of people in order to attract the votes needed to win an election.

FairTax Resources

Here is a list of the resources, organizations, and websites that might be useful to you in your journey to master the FairTax and other personal finance issues.

Additional Resources from Ken Clark

www.collegesavings.about.com

www.themoneytherapist.com

www.twitter.com/PF20

The Complete Idiot's Guide to Boosting Your Financial IQ. Indianapolis: Alpha Books, 2009.

The Complete Idiot's Guide to Getting Out of Debt. Indianapolis: Alpha Books, 2009.

National FairTax Websites

The Pocket Idiot's Guide to the FairTax
Website   www.fairtaxguide.com

Americans for Fair Taxation   www.fairtax.org

The FairTax Blog   www.fairtaxblog.com

FairTax Nation   www.fairtaxnation.com

Zap the IRS Blog   www.zaptheirs.ning.com

State FairTax Websites

Alabama   www.alfairtax.org

Arizona   www.azfairtax.org

Colorado   www.cofairtax.org

Georgia   www.gafairtax.org

Hawaii   www.hifairtax.org

Illinois   www.ilfairtax.org

Indiana   www.fairtaxindiana.net

Kansas   www.ksfairtax.org

Michigan   www.mifairtax.org

Missouri   www.mofairtax.org

Ohio   www.ohfairtax.org

Oklahoma   www.okfairtax.org

Pennsylvania   www.pafairtax.org

New Hampshire   www.nhfairtax.org

North Carolina   www.ncfairtax.org

South Carolina   www.scfairtax.org

Tennessee   www.tnfairtax.org

Wisconsin   www.wifairtax.org

FairTax Books

Boortz, Neal, and John Linder. *The FairTax Book: Saying Goodbye to the IRS and the Income Tax*. New York: Harper Paperbacks, 2005.

———. *FairTax: The Truth: Answering the Critics*. New York: Harper Paperbacks, 2008.

Hewitt, Hugh, and Hank Adler. *The FairTax Fantasy*. Arlington, VA: Townhall Press, 2009.

Morton, Hugh. *The Big Gamble: Dangers of the FairTax*. Baltimore: PublishAmerica, 2008.

Ose, Al. *America's Best Kept Secret: FairTax: Give Yourself a 25% Raise*. Bloomington, IN: AuthorHouse, 2002.

Warwick, Nelson. *FairTax: A Wolf in Sheep's Clothing*. Bloomington, IN: AuthorHouse, 2007.

Index

L

##